Journal on Policy and Complex Systems

Also from Westphalia Press
westphaliapress.org

JOURNAL ON POLICY AND COMPLEX SYSTEMS

Volume 7, Number 2 • Fall 2021

Percy Venegas, Liz Johnson & Joseph Cochran, editors

Westphalia Press
An imprint of Policy Studies Organization

Journal on Policy and Complex Systems
Volume 7, Number 2 • Fall 2021

Westphalia Press
An imprint of Policy Studies Organization
1527 New Hampshire Ave., NW
Washington, D.C. 20036
info@ipsonet.org

ISBN: 978-1-63723-815-8

Cover and interior design by Jeffrey Barnes
jbarnesbook.design

Daniel Gutierrez-Sandoval, Executive Director
PSO and Westphalia Press

Updated material and comments on this edition
can be found at the Westphalia Press website:
www.westphaliapress.org

Journal on Policy and Complex Systems
Volume 7, Number 2 • Fall 2021
© 2022 Policy Studies Organization

JPCS
JOURNAL ON POLICY
AND COMPLEX SYSTEMS

TABLE OF CONTENTS

PSO

Editors & Editorial Board

Submissions may be made by email. There are no publication charges.

For inquiries, please contact Isabel Britez, authors@policyjournal.net

Editor's Letter

Computation has seen many winters in its journey from *promise* to become an instrumental part of scientific research. Hundreds of years passed from the sketches of Leibniz and his mechanical calculators to the fundamental idea of Turing-universal Computation. Interestingly, computational-based research has always seen theorists and practitioners teaming up—what an unlikely pair Babbage and Ada Lovelace were. Even computational architecture theorists like Von Neumann took escapades into the applications realm: *What would it take for an electronic computer to perform numerical weather prediction?* Eventually, scientific computing and complexity science converged—Wolfram and his research on Cellular Automata; Santa Fe Institute Alumni as ambassadors of simulation-based approaches across all over the world; and today, many others relying on Computation to help us model, understand, and devise policy solutions to the challenges of our complex world.

This edition of the *Journal on Policy and Complex Systems* is a testament to the central role that Computation has in the study of complexity today. Each article explores different types of complex systems: socio-technical, physical, even computational. However, the connecting thread is the same: Computation as an enabler of scientific discovery.

Gobet and Venegas model collective cognition and behavior in markets where participants are "internet crowds" and the financial instruments are novel *non-fungible* assets issued in social computers (blockchains), the computational paradigm used is genetic algorithms; their work is relevant to the mandates of regulatory bodies such as the U.S. Securities and Exchange Commission (SEC).

Praddaude, Hogrel, Gay, Baumann, and Bécue tackle issues of practical importance in the intersection of two hot topics: digital manufacturing and cybersecurity. Given the aerospace industry's strategic importance, in alignment with national security interests, this research will appeal both to practitioners in charge of Industry 4.0 initiatives implementation and corporate risk managers overseeing R&D roadmaps.

The complexity of the simulation environment itself becomes a point of concern when dealing with hard computational chemistry problems such as protein folding. With their work, Višňovský, Spišáková, Hozzová, Olha, Trapl, Spiwok, Hejtmánek, and Křenek demonstrate how to tackle the issue of reproducibility of results that affects many high-performance computing (HPC) initiatives. This paper will be a valuable reference to government research agencies and corporations seeking to maximize the return on investment of capital projects that utilize HPC.

doi: 10.18278/jpcs.7.2.1

The problem of workplace adaptation for individuals with disabilities is largely overlooked in our societies. This fact makes timely the research presented here by Surnin, Sitnikov, Gubinkiy, Dorofeev, Nikiforova, Krivosheev, Zemtsov, and Ivaschenko, where artificial intelligence and industrial-grade augmented reality offer practical rehabilitation alternatives in complex human-machine systems. Policymakers will not fail to notice the impact in labor productivity (and therefore GDP) that such simulation approaches could bring.

Papatheodosiou and Angeli bring forth an issue high on the policy agenda: climate risk adaptation and preparedness. The design of complex technological systems in response to critical human needs is of interest to government officials and insurance companies.

Closing the current issue of the Journal we have a paper that expands previous research by the authors on policy and education, and that encompasses the main themes covered in this edition: modeling of human behavior and risk, assistive technology, and online learning, the role of context in modeling complex systems and reproducing results and outcomes. Cochran and Johnson revisit their original work in light of the COVID-19 pandemic, inviting policymakers to reflect on the lessons learned to prepare for the next global emergency.

We could not conclude this introductory motivation without highlighting the multidisciplinary and cross-boundary nature of complexity and scientific computing research. This edition features the work of prominent academics and practitioners from the U.S., Latin America, and Eastern and Western Europe. In view of the current armed conflict in Eastern Europe, let us wish that the spirit of collaboration between scholars serves as an inspiration to pursue peace among the nations of the world.

Best regards,

Percy Venegas

Editor-in-Chief, *Journal on Policy and Complex Systems*

Carta del editor

L a computación ha pasado muchos inviernos en su viaje desde la promesa hasta convertirse en una parte fundamental de la investigación científica. Pasaron cientos de años desde los bocetos de Leibniz y sus calculadoras mecánicas hasta la idea fundamental de la computación universal de Turing. Curiosamente, la investigación basada en computación siempre ha visto a los teóricos y los profesionales formar equipos: qué pareja tan improbable eran Babbage y Ada Lovelace. Incluso los teóricos de la arquitectura computacional como Von Neumann se aventuraron en el ámbito de las aplicaciones: ¿Qué se necesitaría para que una computadora electrónica realizara una predicción meteorológica numérica? Finalmente, la computación científica y la ciencia de la complejidad convergieron: Wolfram y su investigación sobre Autómatas celulares; los exalumnos del Instituto Santa Fe como embajadores de los enfoques basados en la simulación en todo el mundo; y hoy en día, muchos otros confían en Computación para ayudarnos a modelar, comprender y diseñar soluciones de políticas para los desafíos de nuestro mundo complejo.

Esta edición de *Journal on Policy and Complex Systems* es un testimonio del papel central que tiene la computación en el estudio de la complejidad en la actualidad. Cada artículo explora diferentes tipos de sistemas complejos: sociotécnicos, físicos, incluso computacionales. Sin embargo, el hilo conductor es el mismo: la computación como facilitadora del descubrimiento científico.

Gobet y Venegas modelan la cognición y el comportamiento colectivos en mercados donde los participantes son "multitudes de Internet" y los instrumentos financieros son activos no fungibles novedosos emitidos en computadoras sociales (blockchains), el paradigma computacional utilizado son algoritmos genéticos; su trabajo es relevante para los mandatos de los organismos reguladores como la Comisión de Bolsa y Valores de EE. UU. (SEC).

Praddaude, Hogrel, Gay, Baumann y Bécue abordan cuestiones de importancia práctica en la intersección de dos temas candentes: la fabricación digital y la ciberseguridad. Dada la importancia estratégica de la industria aeroespacial, en consonancia con los intereses de seguridad nacional, esta investigación atraerá tanto a los profesionales a cargo de la implementación de iniciativas de la Industria 4.0 como a los administradores de riesgos corporativos que supervisan las hojas de ruta de I+D.

La complejidad del entorno de simulación en sí mismo se convierte en un punto de preocupación cuando se trata de problemas complejos de química computacional como el plegamiento de proteínas. Con su trabajo, Višňovský, Spišáková, Hozzová, Olha, Trapl, Spiwok, Hejtmánek y Křenek demuestran cómo abordar el problema de la reproducibilidad de los resultados que afecta a muchas iniciativas informáticas de alto rendimiento (HPC). Este documento será una referencia valiosa para las agencias de investigación gubernamentales y las corporaciones que buscan maximizar el retorno de la inversión de los proyectos de capital que utilizan HPC.

El problema de la adaptación del lugar de trabajo para las personas con discapacidad se pasa por alto en gran medida en nuestras sociedades. Este hecho hace oportuna la investigación presentada aquí por Surnin, Sitnikov, Gubinkiy, Dorofeev, Nikiforova, Krivosheev, Zemtsov e Ivaschenko, donde la inteligencia artificial y la realidad aumentada de grado industrial ofrecen alternativas prácticas de rehabilitación en sistemas humanos-máquina complejos. Los formuladores de políticas no dejarán de notar el impacto en la productividad laboral (y, por lo tanto, en el PIB) que podrían tener tales enfoques de simulación.

Papatheodosiou y Angeli plantean un tema prioritario en la agenda política: la preparación y la adaptación al riesgo climático. El diseño de sistemas tecnológicos complejos en respuesta a necesidades humanas críticas es de interés para funcionarios gubernamentales y compañías de seguros.

Cerrando el número actual de la revista, tenemos un artículo que amplía la investigación previa de los autores sobre políticas y educación, y que abarca los principales temas tratados en esta edición: modelado del comportamiento humano y el riesgo, tecnología de asistencia y aprendizaje en línea, el papel de contexto en el modelado de sistemas complejos y la reproducción de resultados y resultados. Cochran y Johnson revisan su trabajo original a la luz de la pandemia de COVID-19, invitando a los formuladores de políticas a reflexionar sobre las lecciones aprendidas para prepararse para la próxima emergencia mundial.

No podríamos concluir esta motivación introductoria sin resaltar la naturaleza multidisciplinar y transfronteriza de la complejidad y la investigación en computación científica. Esta edición presenta el trabajo de destacados académicos y profesionales de los EE. UU., América Latina y Europa oriental y occidental. En vista del actual conflicto armado en Europa del Este, deseamos que el espíritu de colaboración entre los estudiosos sirva de inspiración para buscar la paz entre las naciones del mundo.

Saludos,

Percy Venegas

Editor Princial

编者按

计算在从一种迹象到成为科学研究的重要组成部分的历程中经历了许多寒冬。从莱布尼茨的草图和他的机械计算器，到图灵通用计算的基本思想，时间已过去了数百年。有趣的是，基于计算的研究总是由理论家和从业者合作完成——巴贝奇（Babbage）和艾达·洛夫莱斯（Ada Lovelace）的搭档曾是难以置信的。甚至像冯·诺依曼这样的计算结构理论家也在应用领域中尝试冒险：电子计算机需要什么来进行数值天气预报？最终，科学计算和复杂性科学融合在一起——沃尔夫勒姆和他对元胞自动机的研究；圣塔菲研究所校友在世界各地宣传基于模拟的方法；今天，许多人依靠计算来帮助我们建模、理解和设计应对复杂世界挑战的政策解决方案。

本期《政策与复杂系统杂志》证明了计算在当今复杂性研究中的中心作用。每篇文章都探究了不同类型的复杂系统：社会技术系统、物理系统，甚至是计算系统。不过，相连接的主线是一样的：计算作为科学发现的推动者。

Gobet和Venegas对市场中的集体认知和行为进行建模，在这些市场中，参与者是"互联网群体"，金融工具是社会计算机（区块链）中发行的新型"非同质化"资产，使用的计算范式是遗传算法；这篇文章对美国证券交易委员会（SEC）等监管机构的授权具有相关性。

Praddaude、Hogrel、Gay、Baumann和Bécue研究了数字制造和网络安全这两个热门话题的交叉所存在的具有实际重要性的问题。鉴于航空航天业的战略重要性，并与国家安全利益相一致，这项研究将吸引负责工业4.0倡议实施的从业者以及监督研发路线图的企业风险管理者。

在处理诸如蛋白质折叠等计算化学难题时，模拟环境本身的复杂性成为一个关注点。在论文中，Višňovský、Spišáková、Hozzová、Olha、Trapl、Spiwok、Hejtmánek和 Křenek展示了如何应对结果可重复性这一问题，其能影响许多高性能计算（HPC）倡议。本文将为政府研究机构和公司提供有价值的参考，这些机构和公司试图将使用HPC的资本项目的投资回报最大化。

我们的社会在很大程度上忽视了残障人士的工作场所适应问题。这一事实使得 Surnin、Sitnikov、Gubinkiy、Dorofeev、Nikiforova、Krivosheev、Zemtsov 和 Ivaschenko提出的研究具有及时性，研究描述了人工智能和工业级增强现实在复杂的人机系统中所提供的实用康复替代方案。政策制定者不会忽视这种模拟方法可能对劳动生产率（以及GDP）产生的影响。

Papatheodosiou和Angeli提出了政策议程中的一个重要问题：气候风险适应和准备。响应关键人类需求的复杂技术系统的设计是政府官员和保险公司的兴趣所在。

本期收录的最后一篇论文对政策教育学者的以往研究加以扩展，涵盖了本期涉及的主题：人类行为和风险建模、辅助技术和网络学习、以及情境在复杂系统建模和重复结果中的作用。鉴于COVID-19大流行，Cochran和Johnson重新审视了他们的原创研究，邀请决策者反思经验教训，为下一次全球紧急情况作准备。

如果不强调复杂性和科学计算研究的多学科性质和跨界性质，我们就无法为本篇社论作结论。本期收录了来自美国、拉丁美洲以及东西欧著名学者和从业者的研究。鉴于当前东欧的武装冲突，我们希望学者之间的合作精神成为世界各国追求和平的灵感。

献上最好的祝福，
Percy Venegas 《政策与复杂系统杂志》主编

Journal on Policy and Complex Systems • Volume 7, Number 2 • Fall 2021

Modeling NFT Investor Behavior Using Belief Dissensus

Percy Venegas
King's College London/Economy Monitor

Fernand Gobet
London School of Economics and Political Science

Acknowledgements: We thank SimilarWeb Ltd for access to web panel data at the US state level.

Abstract

Investment into non-fungible tokens (NFTs) has skyrocketed in 2021. Since NFTs are issued on blockchains, the underlying operation is that of a social computer—therefore, modeling social cognition in NFT markets becomes relevant. Market participants (collectors, speculators, and investors) may display different levels of expertise that serve as "social labels." However, do users of NFT marketplaces care about price or community? Besides the operational consensus mechanism of the blockchain (which also provides the hard judiciary and settlement layers of the system), we must consider the soft consensus of the internet communities that drive their attention towards NFT marketplaces where the monetary assets are listed. In this research note, we propose an approach that offers a window on human cognition and collective intelligence, but that can inform the development of artificial systems that help develop policies to protect the public interest of investors.

Keywords: non-fungible tokens, NFTs, cryptomarkets, evolutionary algorithms, cognitive science

Modelar el comportamiento de los inversores NFT utilizando el desacuerdo de creencias

Resumen

La inversión en tokens no fungibles (NFT) se disparó en 2021. Dado que los NFT se emiten en cadenas de bloques, la operación subyacente es la

doi: 10.18278/jpcs.7.2.2

de una computadora social; por lo tanto, el modelado de la cognición social en los mercados de NFT se vuelve relevante. Los participantes del mercado (coleccionistas, especuladores e inversores) pueden mostrar diferentes niveles de experiencia que sirven como "etiquetas sociales". Sin embargo, ¿a los usuarios de los mercados NFT les importa el precio o la comunidad? Además del mecanismo de consenso operativo de la cadena de bloques (que también proporciona las capas judiciales y de liquidación duras del sistema), debemos considerar el consenso blando de las comunidades de Internet que dirigen su atención hacia los mercados NFT donde se enumeran los activos monetarios. En esta nota de investigación, proponemos un enfoque que ofrece una ventana a la cognición humana y la inteligencia colectiva, pero que puede informar el desarrollo de sistemas artificiales que ayuden a desarrollar políticas para proteger el interés público de los inversores.

Palabras clave: tokens no fungibles, NFT, criptomercados, algoritmos evolutivos, ciencia cognitiva

使用信念岐见对非同质化代币投资者行为进行建模

摘要

对非同质化代币（NFTs）的投资在2021年激增。鉴于NFT在区块链上发行，潜在的操作则是社会计算机操作，因此，对NFT市场中的社会认知进行建模一事便具有相关性。市场参与者（收集者、投机者和投资者）可能展现不同程度的专业性，这种专业性充当不同的"社会标签"。不过，NFT市场用户真的关心价格或社区吗？除了区块链的操作共识机制（为该系统提供稳固的司法层面和解决层面），我们必须衡量互联网社区的软共识，该社区将关注转向将货币资产包括在内的NFT市场。在该研究纪要中，我们提出一项措施，该措施为人类认知和集体智慧提供窗口，并能影响人工系统的开发，帮助发展一系列保护投资者公共利益的政策。

关键词：非同质化代币，NFTs，加密货币市场，演化算法，认知科学

Introduction

The technology behind non-fungible tokens (NFTs) has been around since 2017, but interest in NFTs as collectives and investable assets only gained traction during 2021, with sales over USD 10 Billion in 2021 (see Table 1).

Table 1. *NFT market size. Source: Nonfungible.com*

Key figures of NFT market as of November 12, 2021	All-time as of November 12 2021	Last 30 days as of November 12 2021
Sales value	10.2bn USD	1.69bn USD
Primary sales value	2.35bn USD	0.43bn USD
Secondary sales value	7.84bn USD	1.26bn USD
Average sales value	927.71 USD	1831.41 USD
Number of sales	10.99 million	0.92 million
Active market wallets	799623	241337
Unique buyers	756135	215227
Unique sellers	304798	88969

Effectively, NFTs are tokens that provide access to communities of like-minded investors. Those subcultures not only become investable but also offer an intrinsic rewards system. In their paper on social identification and investment decisions, Bauer and Smeets (2015) argue that investors get non-financial utility if investments fit their (desired) social identity. However, to what extent are NFT investors interested in community versus only prices?

Expertise theory

Nadini et al. (2021) have studied traders and NFTs networks and found that most traders are specialized: measuring how individuals distribute their trades across collections, they found that at least 73% of traders' transactions are performed in their top collection, and at least 82% in their top two collections. Such studies that use exchange and marketplace data indeed shed light on the microeconomics of the market. However, to understand the market operation at the macroeconomic level, it is necessary to use off-chain data.

A prevalent albeit imperfect definition of expertise considers *expertise as experience*—that is, the achievement of expert status is related to the amount of time an individual has spent in a domain (Gobet, 2016). Table 2 shows the estimated visit duration in minutes at the site Opensea.io, one of the largest NFT marketplaces in the world. There are two interesting observations to make: first, we can confirm an increase in interest during the last half of 2021;

second, time spent on the site increased prominently among desktop users. Professional and semi-professional investors are desktop users, so having the time on site doubling from May to August is a strong indication of increased expertise.

Table 2. *Visit duration to Opensea.io (hours: mins: secs), source: Similarweb*

Date	Avg. Visit Duration (Mobile Web)	Avg. Visit Duration (Desktop)
01/12/2019	00:02:36	00:09:00
01/01/2020	00:02:06	00:11:39
01/02/2020	00:01:46	00:09:47
01/03/2020	00:01:12	00:11:59
01/04/2020	00:00:56	00:10:19
01/05/2020	00:01:31	00:11:37
01/06/2020	00:01:20	00:08:12
01/07/2020	00:01:20	00:09:16
01/08/2020	00:01:13	00:09:50
01/09/2020	00:01:02	00:07:15
01/10/2020	00:01:25	00:11:13
01/11/2020	00:01:04	00:07:14
01/12/2020	00:01:00	00:07:11
01/01/2021	00:01:09	00:09:15
01/02/2021	00:01:14	00:09:50
01/03/2021	00:01:24	00:10:26
01/04/2021	00:01:13	00:08:59
01/05/2021	00:01:26	00:11:09
01/06/2021	00:01:40	00:14:19

01/07/2021	00:01:40	00:16:54
01/08/2021	00:02:01	00:20:22
01/09/2021	00:01:46	00:19:08
01/10/2021	00:01:41	00:17:29
01/11/2021	00:01:48	00:14:07
01/12/2021	00:01:40	00:14:43
01/01/2022	00:02:02	00:17:39

However, deliberate practice (Ericsson et al., 1993) offers a better measure to understand the acquisition of expertise. Deliberate practice is systematic, focused, and seeks to improve performance. Specialization from this perspective means that the new NFT traders, many technically savvy, had to peruse financial sites (many of which were specialized in crypto) to improve their financial literacy and execute their trading activities. The concentration of topics into finance and technology in Figure 1 confirms this assertion.

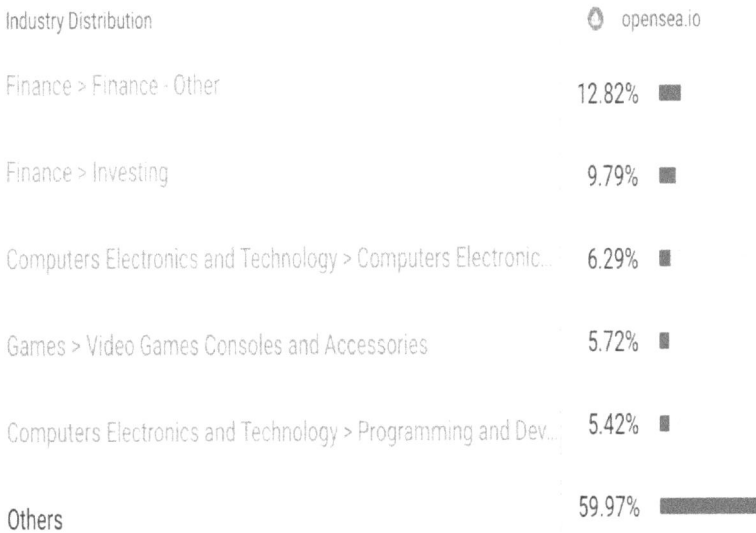

Industry Distribution		opensea.io
Finance > Finance - Other	12.82%	
Finance > Investing	9.79%	
Computers Electronics and Technology > Computers Electronic...	6.29%	
Games > Video Games Consoles and Accessories	5.72%	
Computers Electronics and Technology > Programming and Dev...	5.42%	
Others	59.97%	

Figure 1. Distribution of site categories visited by the audience of Opensea.io in the U.S. from Dec 2020 to Nov 2021. Source: Similarweb.

Nevertheless, "expertise" can often only be used within a specific context (Stein, 1997). Therefore, we also explore geographical social groups across the United States.

The study

To investigate the response of market participants to movements in price and popularity of NFTs, we use alternative data. Prices are denominated in USD and come from the NFT Index by https://nftindex.tech/, an index that tracks the performance of tokens within the NFT industry. The index is capitalization-weighted and tracks the market performance of decentralized financial assets, if they are significantly used and committed to ongoing maintenance and development. The index tracks assets available in the Ethereum blockchain and is independent of any marketplace, making it suitable for macro-level price monitoring, i.e., keeping the pulse of the NFT markets.

We use the estimated average number of daily pages visited in Opensea.io across a group of U.S. States (Arizona, California, Florida, Georgia, Illinois, Massachusetts, Michigan, New Jersey, New York, North Carolina, Ohio, Pennsylvania, Texas, Virginia, and Washington), since an increment on pages visited signals increased interest and adoption. Assets listed in Opensea are issued as ERC-721 standard compliant, which means that they are predominantly issued on the Ethereum blockchain and priced in Ether.

We use total pages visited on the site https://www.airnfts.com/ as a proxy for the popularity of NFT collectives. To prevent the evolutionary algorithm (see below) from feeding on a self-reinforcing bias, we choose a site operating on a platform different from Ethereum, which should remove at least part of the possible audience overlap. AirNFTs lists assets issued in the Binance Blockchain; Binance is the largest exchange globally in terms of the daily trading volume of cryptocurrencies (Peters, 2021).

The dataset contains daily observations between April 19th and November 30th, 2021. Similarweb.com provides web panel (visits) data. The data exploration and modeling phases are performed using Mathematica (Wolfram Research, 2021) and Datamodeler (Evolved Analytics, 2021). The dataset is available for download at: https://www.autonomous.economymonitor.com/s/NFT-master.csv

Methodology

We start with exploratory data analysis to understand the shape of the data: the main statistical properties and correlations between variables. Then, the modeling stage is done using symbolic regression via genetic programming, a technique that has previously been used to study crypto-economic systems (Venegas, 2021). There are two rounds of modeling: the first round is performed mainly to discover the driver variables (this focus helps the evolutionary algorithm find and develop creative paths, rather than losing time with spurious associations between variables); the second round consists in building groups of models ("ensembles") with explanatory and predictive power. This workflow is repeated for each of the two target variables: price and popularity. Finally, a multi-target modeling stage is introduced. Here, we compare ensembles of diverse, optimal models (both accurate and simple).

The general idea is straightforward: if people's beliefs in *price appreciation* and *popularity increase* reach consensus, their browsing activity should intensify. Moreover, where there is dissensus and increasing uncertainty, the choice of predictive variables should be revisited.

Results

Descriptive Statistics

The main statistical properties of the dataset are analyzed (Figure 2). We find that all numerical variables are continuous, and observations are uniform (records are complete 92% of the time and above). The values are strictly positive (no zero-crosses).

DataSummaryTable

Col	Label	Type	Uniformity	Class	Unique	Distribution Plot	Zero–Cross	Min	Mean	Median	Max
1	Date	ABC	100%	⬭	226	Lots of different values	⊕	10/10/2021	9/9/2021	9/9/2021	9/9/2021
2	Arizona	123	99%	∿	220		↦	1.0	30.8	21.7	222.8
3	California	123	100%	∿	217		↦	4.3	18.0	17.4	40.2
4	Florida	123	100%	∿	215		↦	3.0	18.3	16.8	61.1
5	Georgia	123	100%	∿	213		↦	1.0	13.6	12.3	52.8
6	Illinois	123	100%	∿	214		↦	2.9	15.2	12.1	175.6
7	Massachusetts	123	100%	∿	214		↦	1.0	16.6	14.9	76.3
8	Michigan	123	99%	∿	215		↦	1.0	13.8	11.6	58.8
9	New Jersey	123	100%	∿	215		↦	2.5	18.8	17.3	62.1
10	New York	123	100%	∿	212		↦	3.1	15.2	14.8	44.1
11	North Carolina	123	100%	∿	219		↦	1.8	27.8	19.3	181.4
12	Ohio	123	92%	∿	199		↦	1.0	14.2	10.5	69.5
13	Pennsylvania	123	100%	∿	213		↦	2.3	26.2	21.4	119.8
14	Texas	123	100%	∿	212		↦	2.6	14.7	14.1	58.1
15	Virginia	123	100%	∿	212		↦	2.0	13.5	12.4	62.7
16	Washington	123	100%	∿	212		↦	1.2	13.8	12.5	54.9
17	Price	123	100%	∿	225		↦	354.3	863.2	706.2	1643.3
18	Popularity	123	98%	∿	222		↦	61.0	5467.7	3963.7	34845.0

Figure 2. Data summary table with the main statistical properties of the dataset. Own construction using Datamodeler; Source: Similarweb and NFTindex.tech.

DataDistributionPlot

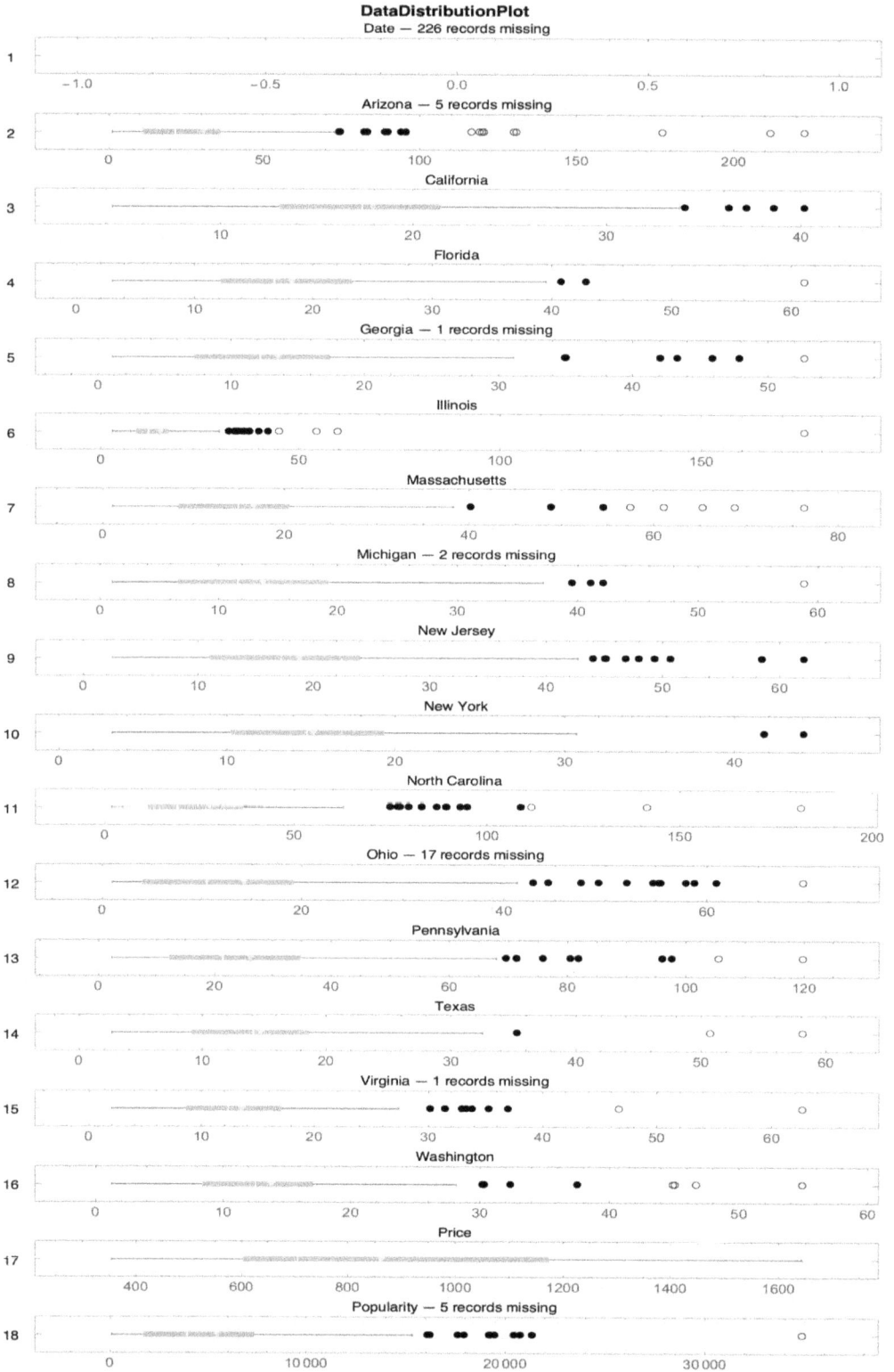

Figure 3. Central values and dispersion for each variable. Own construction using Datamodeler; Source: Similarweb and NFTindex.tech.

Data distribution

The dispersion of the data is different between states. For instance, in Ohio, the 75th percentile is 19.295 with a peak at 69.47, while in Illinois, it is 17.25 with a large outlier at 175.59. This may point to different user behavior across regions in the U.S., or perhaps some data mining experiments being conducted at locations (typically, such experimentation would be conducted using bots, which could generate large volumes of "artificial" activity that may skew the data). The box and whisker plots in Figure 3 depict the spread and locali-

ty of data points, with the data within the 25% and 75% percentiles shown in orange, the median as a white dent in the orange bar, and the mean as a green marker; the black dots are outliers, and the white dots are far outliers.

Timeseries

The timeseries plots (Figure 4) provide a sense of the shape of the data. Here we confirm how marketplace usage behavior seems to vary significantly across states. Also, we see the first hints of an apparent decoupling of price and popularity.

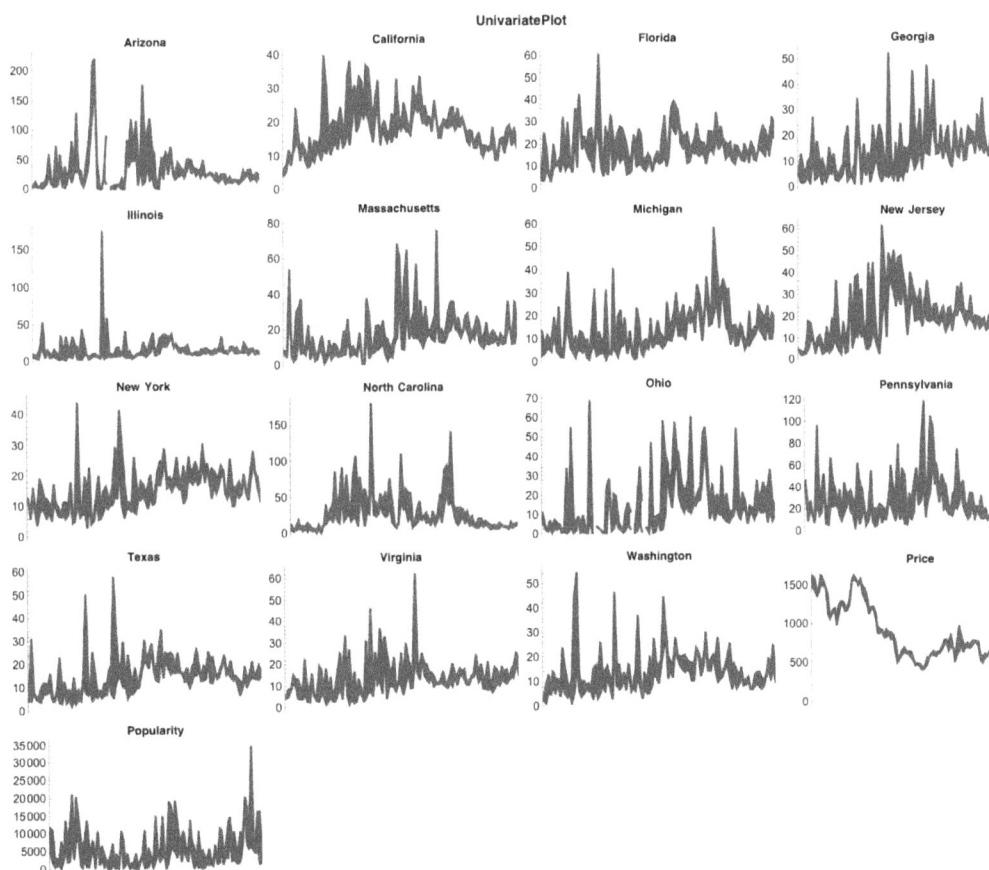

Figure 4. Univariate plots (X axis is time, Y axis is values of each variable). Own construction using Datamodeler; Source: Similarweb and NFTindex.tech.

Correlations

The linear correlations between variables confirm the previous observation regarding the relationship between price and popularity (negative correla-tion) and between price and the other variables. For instance, we note that at a 0.4 threshold, the price is negatively correlated to site activity in Texas and New York (Figure 5).

Correlation Chart (price)

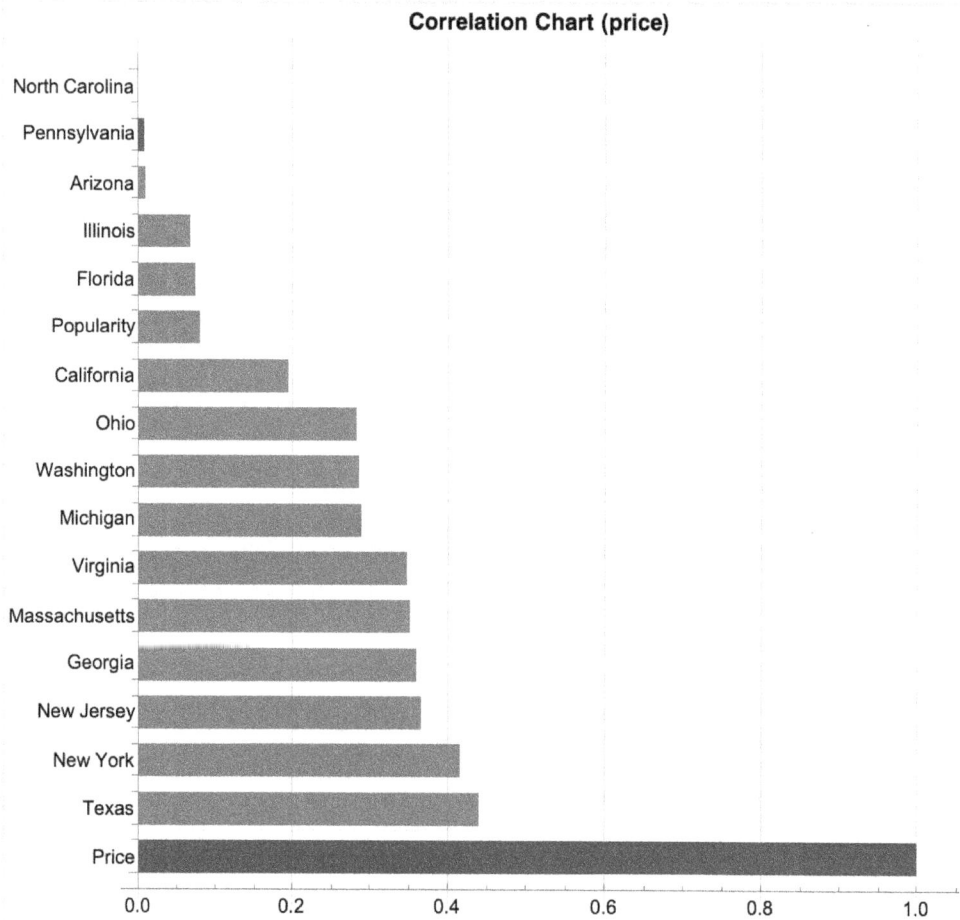

Figure 5. Absolute correlations with price. Positive correlations in blue; negative correlations in red. Own construction using Datamodeler; Source data: Similarweb and NFTindex.tech.

Modeling

<u>First round.</u> During the first modeling round, we developed 1,138 models for price and 971 for popularity. We discover the more prevalent variables across models in each case (depicted in Figure 6 and 7 as predominantly solid red bars): for the price, marketplace site activity in New Jersey, New York, Ohio, and Texas; for popularity, New Jersey, North Carolina, and Ohio. The interpretation of the figures is as follow: in each model (X axis) a variable will

be present (or not)—the variables that present higher visual density are likely to be more important.

Second round. For the second modeling round, we create a subset with the variables in common, Ohio and New Jersey. We then run the second round of modeling using the same modeling parameters (i.e., types of mathematical blocks) but only that new subset of variables. As we will see below, the number of total models generated in this case is different: the reason is that once the evolutionary algorithm is constrained to work with fewer variables, it can itself specialize and develop new populations of models.

Price

Figure 8 shows the 11 models included in the ensemble, out of 1,099 models developed in the second round. The red dots in the "knee" of the pareto denote models that have a good balance between complexity and accuracy.

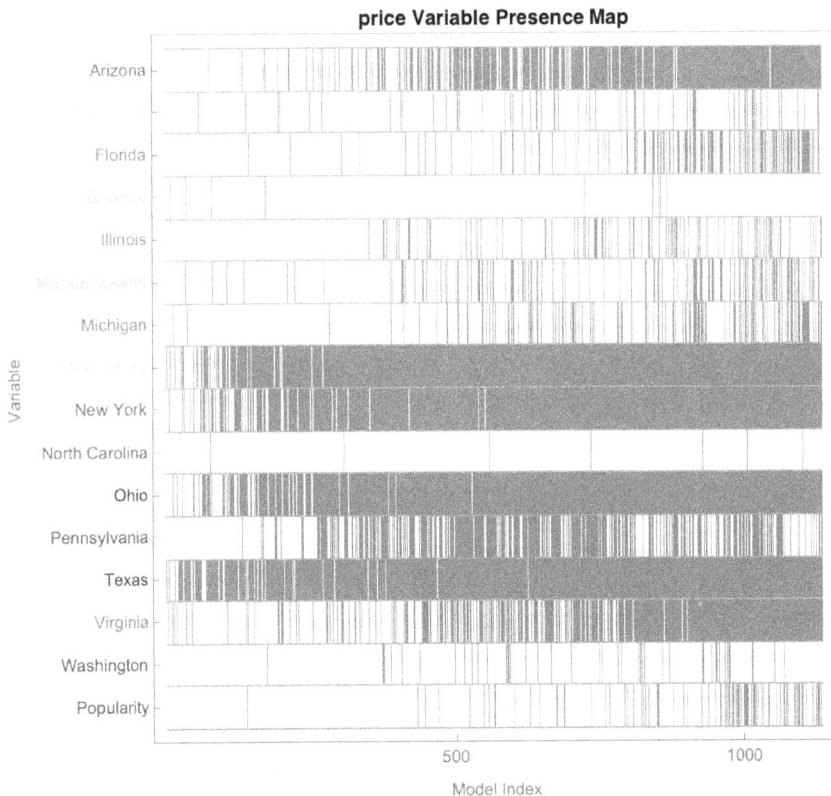

Figure 6. Variable presence across models (target: price).
Own construction using Datamodeler.

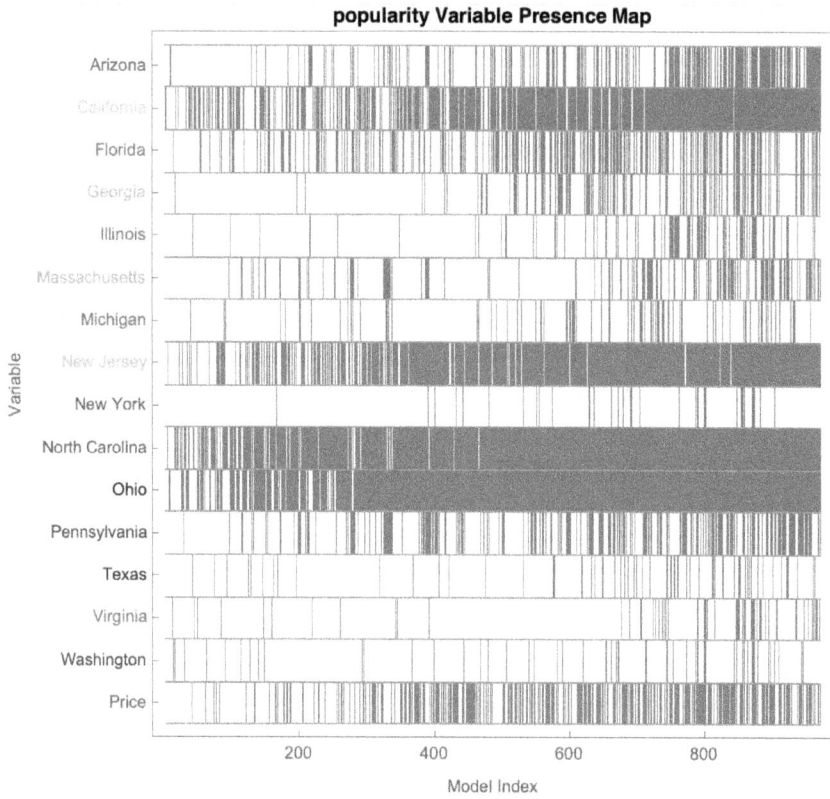

Figure 7. Variable presence across models (target: popularity).
Own construction using Datamodeler.

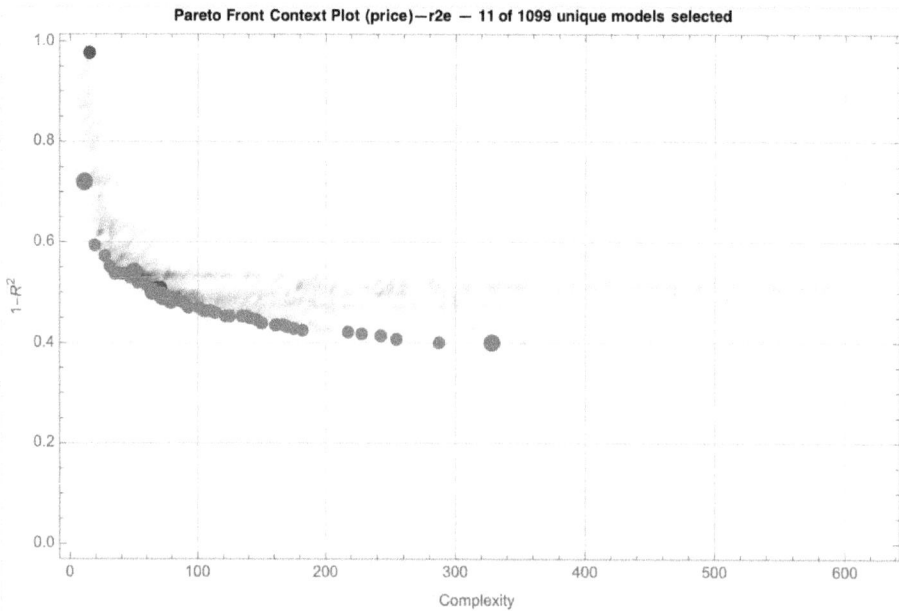

Figure 8. Accuracy – Complexity trade-off (price). Gray dots
are suboptimal models, not included in the ensemble.

In Figure 9, the models are ranked by complexity and error.

Model Selection Report (price)

	Complexity	$1-R^2$	Function
1	11	0.720	$653.23 + \dfrac{2510.90}{}$
2	15	0.979	$889.59 - (1.74 \times 10^{-3})^{3}$
3	50	0.540	$879.34 + \dfrac{9783.15}{7.64+} - 247.59\sqrt{\text{Ohio}} + 20.40\,\text{Ohio} + 0.25 \qquad \text{Ohio}$
4	65	0.503	$459.72 + \dfrac{14207.95}{9.27+} - 50.78\,\text{Ohio} + 1.00 \qquad \text{Ohio} + 0.88\,\text{Ohio}^2 - (3.60 \times 10^{-4}) \qquad \text{Ohio}^3$
5	69	0.509	$3323.25 - 203.11\sqrt{} - \dfrac{724.93}{\text{Ohio}} - 911.14\sqrt{\text{Ohio}} + 94.07\,\text{Ohio} + 1.84 \qquad \text{Ohio} - (3.49 \times 10^{-2}) \qquad \text{Ohio}^2$
6	71	0.507	$937.45 - \dfrac{35559.62}{4} + \dfrac{3874.54}{} + 3.45 \qquad - \dfrac{7.84}{-9.10+} - 235.55\sqrt{\text{Ohio}} + 24.13\,\text{Ohio}$
7	72	0.497	$2584.80 - 1187.19^{1/3} + 49.07 \qquad - \dfrac{70.01}{\text{Ohio}} + 6.42\,\text{Ohio} + \dfrac{4271.79}{21+\text{Ohio}}$
8	73	0.491	$1549.98 + \dfrac{14902.05}{9.73+} - \dfrac{546.08}{\text{Ohio}} - 725.95\sqrt{\text{Ohio}} + 76.34\,\text{Ohio} + 1.33 \qquad \text{Ohio} - (2.62 \times 10^{-2}) \qquad \text{Ohio}^2$
9	73	0.492	$1581.21 + \dfrac{11770.18}{7.64+} - \dfrac{519.54}{\text{Ohio}} - 700.49\sqrt{\text{Ohio}} + 74.00\,\text{Ohio} + 1.24 \qquad \text{Ohio} - (2.49 \times 10^{-2}) \qquad \text{Ohio}^2$
10	80	0.485	$2736.75 - \dfrac{419.14}{} + 2.49 \qquad \text{Ohio} + 0.40\,\text{Ohio}^2 - (3.64 \times 10^{-2}) \qquad \text{Ohio}^2 - 660.68(\qquad \text{Ohio})^{1/4}$
11	328	0.399	$-96944.59 - 585.05\sqrt{} + 28.35 \qquad + \dfrac{4766.58}{42.60+2} \dfrac{}{+\frac{-6+\text{Ohio}}{-6+\text{Ohio}}+3} \dfrac{}{\sqrt{\text{Ohio}}} - 894.54\sqrt{\text{Ohio}} +$ $8.65 \qquad \sqrt{\text{Ohio}} + 112.27\,\text{Ohio} - \dfrac{468.31\,\text{Ohio}}{27.53+\frac{}{-6+\text{Ohio}}}^2 - (2.18 \times 10^{-2}) \qquad \text{Ohio}^2 + \dfrac{7856043.60}{\left(8.82+\frac{}{9.07+}+3\right)^{}\sqrt{\text{Ohio}+\text{Ohio}^3}}$

Figure 9. Ensemble constituent models (price) from lower to higher complexity.

In Figure 10, the range of embedded model predictions is shown in blue, while the modeling outliers (most difficult data records to model) are shown in red. We note that the prediction performance is more challenging at higher price levels.

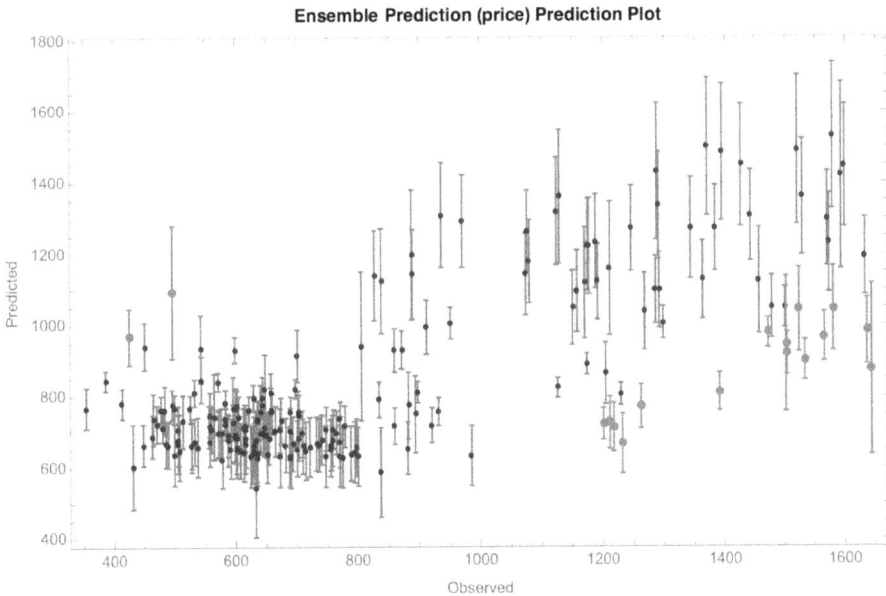

Ensemble Prediction (price) Prediction Plot

Figure 10. Ensemble performance (price). The range of computed values is represented by the length of the lines.

Popularity

In the second round, we developed 1000 models for popularity; Figure 11 shows the 11 models selected for the ensemble.

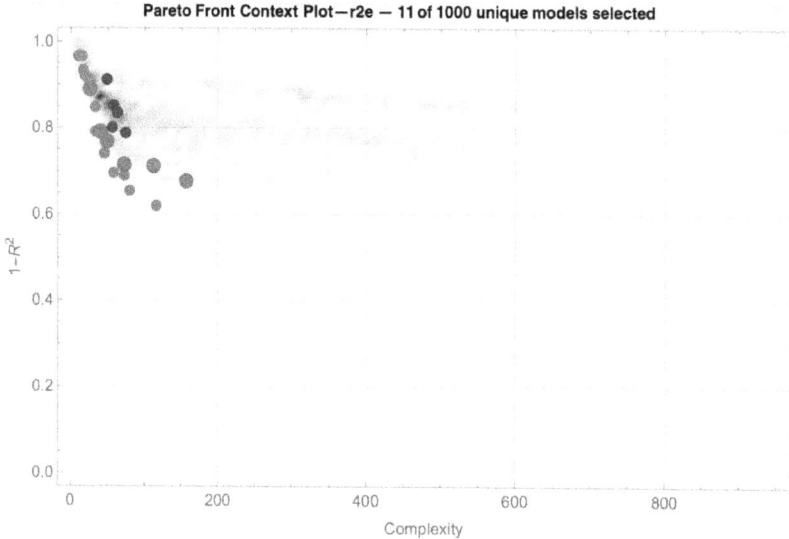

Figure 11. Accuracy-complexity trade-off (popularity). Gray dots are suboptimal models, not included in the ensemble.

The models are again ranked by complexity and error (Figure 12). We note some peculiarities: how the minimum complexity for the popularity models (27) is higher than in the case of the price models (11) and how the minimum error (0.889 vs. 0.720) is also higher.

Model Selection Report (popularity)

	Complexity	$1-R^2$	Function
1	27	0.889	$7534.11 - 109.90 \text{ New Jersey} + \frac{925.92}{-10.44 + \text{Ohio}}$
2	41	0.792	$7519.61 - 114.81 \text{ New Jersey} - \frac{769.51}{7.22 + \text{New Jersey} - 2\text{ Ohio}}$
3	49	0.767	$6860.81 - 125.75 \text{ New Jersey} - \frac{766.52}{7.22 + \text{New Jersey} - 2\text{ Ohio}} + 60.57 \text{ Ohio}$
4	49	0.912	$4381.26 - 217.07 \text{ New Jersey} + 807.80 \left(\text{New Jersey}^2\right)^{1/4} + 551.61 \sqrt{\text{Ohio}}$
5	57	0.800	$4532.09 - \frac{678.23}{7.22 + \text{New Jersey} - 2\text{ Ohio}} + \frac{1057.97}{14.08 - \text{Ohio}} + 52.59 \text{ Ohio}$
6	59	0.850	$5036.89 - \frac{399.99}{10 - \text{Ohio}} + 37.74 \text{ Ohio} - \frac{153.92}{-0.96 + \text{Ohio}} + \frac{926.17}{-10.44 + \text{Ohio}}$
7	63	0.835	$6605.89 - 109.52 \text{ New Jersey} - \frac{1553.36}{-8.27 + \text{New Jersey}} - \frac{1898.19}{\text{Ohio}} + 406.82 \sqrt{\text{Ohio}} - \frac{68.77}{-0.95 + \text{Ohio}}$
8	73	0.714	$7560.14 - 122.85 \text{ New Jersey} - \frac{756.92}{7.22 + \text{New Jersey} - 2\text{ Ohio}} - \frac{16.17}{0.95 - \text{Ohio}} - \frac{2673.49}{\text{Ohio}} + 39.54 \text{ Ohio}$
9	75	0.788	$9856.54 - 167.29 \text{ New Jersey} - \frac{422.62}{10 - \text{Ohio}} - \frac{143.55}{-0.96 + \text{Ohio}} + \frac{877.00}{-10.44 + \text{Ohio}} - \frac{25912.89}{\text{New Jersey} + \text{Ohio}}$
10	112	0.712	$-14020.79 + \frac{206646.27}{8.61 - \frac{1}{8.61 - \text{New Jersey}}} - \frac{15793.38}{\text{New Jersey}} - 173.69 \text{ New Jersey} - \frac{597.47}{7.08 + \text{New Jersey} + \frac{2}{\text{Ohio}} - 2\text{ Ohio}} + \frac{945.45}{14.08 - \text{Ohio}}$
11	157	0.676	$-8731.16 + \frac{161521.57}{8.61 - \frac{1}{8.61 - \text{New Jersey}}} - 154.53 \text{ New Jersey} - \frac{649.52}{7.08 + \text{New Jersey} + \frac{2}{\text{Ohio}} - 2\text{ Ohio}} - \frac{2543.36}{\text{Ohio}} - \frac{47656.99}{\text{New Jersey} + 3\text{ Ohio} + \frac{1}{-\sqrt{\text{Ohio}} + \text{Ohio}^2}}$

Figure 12. Ensemble constituent models (popularity) from lower to higher complexity.

The ensemble prediction tends to have a better performance at lower popularity levels (Figure 13), with a large dispersion at the peak point—where a single traffic spike occurred, as seen previously in Fig 5.

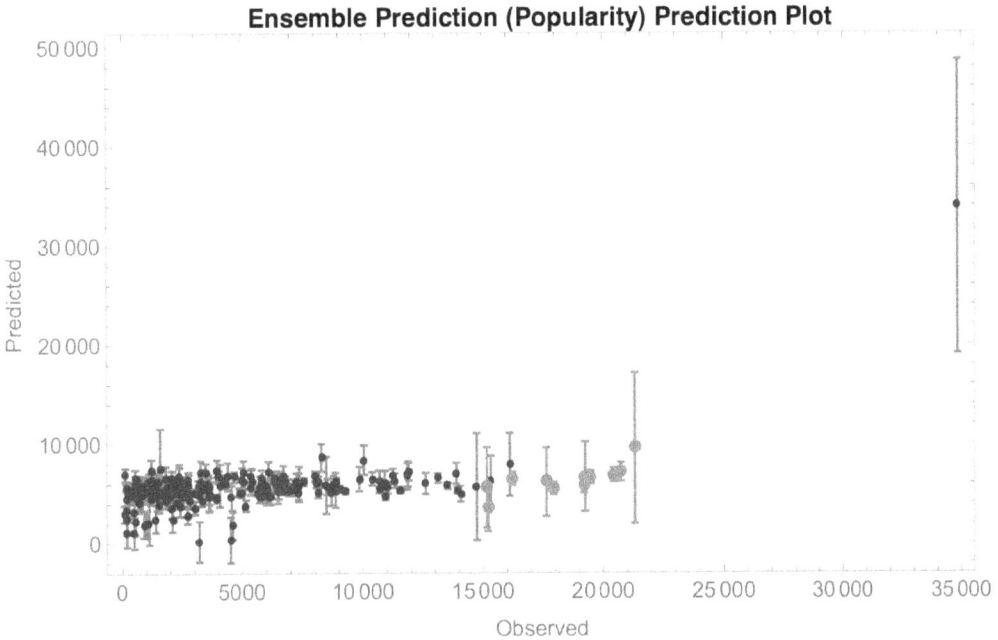

Ensemble Prediction (Popularity) Prediction Plot

Figure 13. Ensemble performance (popularity). The range of computed values is represented by the length of the lines.

Multi-target response

Finally, we analyze the responses for the variables that are common to both model ensembles (New Jersey and Ohio). The explorer in Figure 14 allows us to see the effect of changing parameter values simultaneously on multiple target behaviors.

The trade-off curves move from red (minimum) to green (maximum) values of daily visits in each state. Normally, we would expect a curve with no loops or discontinuities; however, in this case we notice possible pathologies in the models (specially for popularity).

A closer inspection of the individual price (C.1 and C.2) and popularity (D.1 and D.2) response plots shows how the dissensus of models is predictable around mean values (blue line) with bounds defined by an envelope (yellow ribbon) and constituent models (ensemble submodels) depicted as gray lines inside the ribbon. In the case of price, we see a few instances when the submodels go outside of the boundaries, but mostly they remain within the ribbon. Popularity, however, is harder to model—there are several input values for which an output prediction value would be undefined (seen as pronounced spikes in the ribbon).

This difficulty in modeling the system when optimizing for popularity is consistent with the choice of variables: we should expect dissociation of behavior since the users are specialized in different blockchains (Ethereum and Binance Blockchain) which are largely mutually exclusive in terms of technology and user community. To be sure, modeling price is not without challenge: the size of the ribbon widens even for small values of pages visited (e.g., 20) which indicates an increase in uncertainty.

Revisiting the site categories of Figure 1, but this time at the local level (as shown in Fig 15 and 16), we find that the distribution of categories for the sites visited by the audience of the marketplace differ: in Ohio, it is predominantly technology and social network sites (like Discord, Twitter, Medium and Reddit), while in New Jersey it is mainly Other types of Financial sites (like crypto finance, such as Coinbase and Coingecko). This makes sense considering that the users in New Jersey are closer to the large financial center of New York City, and likely many of them work in the financial industry or are connected with people who do. On the other hand, users in Ohio might be predominantly in the early stages of their exposure to NFT markets (in the phase of discovery via social networks) – and, with less exposure to the financial industry, their level of interest in the financial aspects of NFT assets might be lower than in the case of users from New Jersey.

By the fact that C.1 and C.2 have conventional shapes (models diverge around a mean across different values of the parameter space), while D.1 and D.2 contain singularities, we confirm that the intensity of site activity (as expressed by pages per visit) is a better predictor of price than a predictor of popularity. The uncertainty of the prediction itself changes, with minimal uncertainty (narrower ribbons) around the value of 40 pages per visit in New Jersey and 55 in Ohio.

This behavior is precisely what we should expect given the selection of target variables: NFT investors in Opensea mainly use the Ethereum blockchain, and users of AirNFTs mainly use the Binance Blockchain – in other words, they belong to separate technology networks and effectively different communities. While both A and B show abnormal shapes (typically the relationship between two variables that are prevalent across models, when a third dimension is encoded in color, would be more similar to an arc), the discontinuity in B confirms again that price and popularity are disassociated when the groups of users are different, especially in Ohio.

The results suggest that price and popularity can be modeled meaningfully only within the same community (users of the same technology or NFT-issuing blockchain network). It also shows that the prediction accuracy varies with changing levels of activity in different geographical locations, which suggests that NFT investors' behavior is modulated by cyberspace and physical space factors.

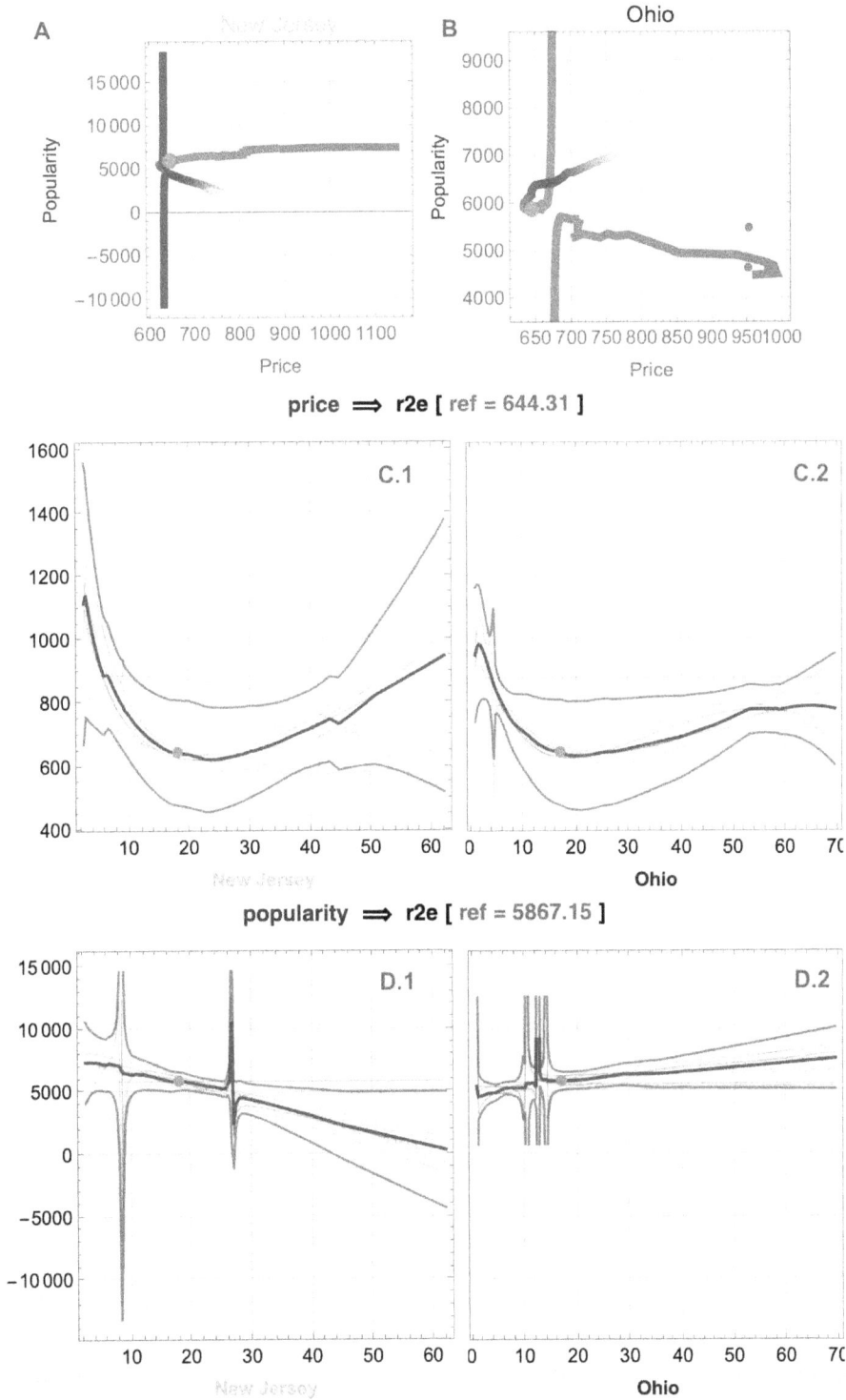

Figure 14. Multi-target response explorer. A) Trade-off curve for variable Ohio; A) Trade-off curve for variable New Jersey; C.1, C.2) Response plots for target: price; D.1, D.2) Response plots for target: popularity.

Industry Distribution		opensea.io
Computers Electronics and Technology > Social Networks and Online Com...	16.06%	
Finance > Investing	11.00%	
Finance > Finance - Other	10.20%	
Computers Electronics and Technology > Computers Electronics and Tech...	7.59%	
Computers Electronics and Technology > Programming and Developer Soft...	6.81%	
Others	48.34%	

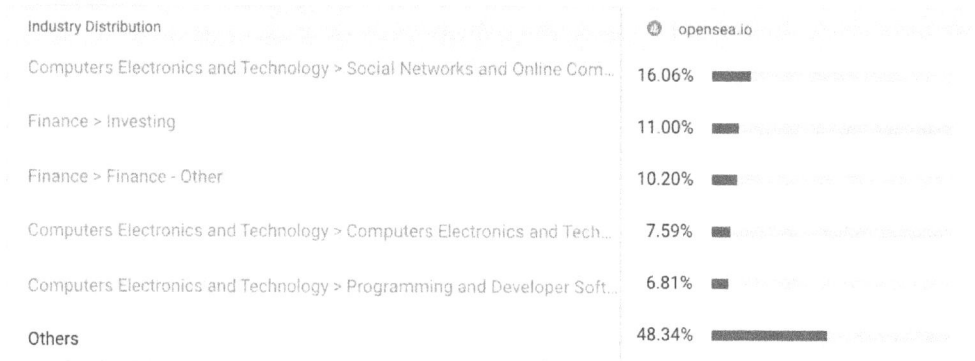

Figure 15. Audience preferences in Ohio, Opensea.io Dec 2020-Nov 2021.

Industry Distribution		opensea.io
Finance > Finance - Other	12.08%	
Finance > Investing	10.88%	
Computers Electronics and Technology > Computers Electronics and Tech...	7.88%	
News and Media	7.68%	
Computers Electronics and Technology > Social Networks and Online Com...	6.68%	
Others	54.80%	

Figure 16. Audience preferences in New Jersey, Opensea.io Dec 2020-Nov 2021.

Conclusions

We found that NFT market participant behavior differs across different states in the U.S. Market beliefs on price and popularity (expressed as changes in activity in the off-chain marketplace) are indicators of interest and a strong precursor of economic activity.

A definitive classification of motivations among possible extremes, i.e., purely speculative or community-driven, will require the analysis of other facets besides grouping at the regional level. However, we confirmed that expertise resides both in the expert and a social system: users in different states also have different priorities regarding topics of interest related to financial literacy. A future study may cover the relationship between the general popularity of collectives and the degree of specialization of marketplace users in financial topics.

References

Bauer, R., & Smeets, P. (2015). Social identification and investment decisions. *Journal of Economic Behavior & Organization, 117*(C), 121-134, https://EconPapers. repec.org/RePEc:eee:jeborg:v:117:y:2015:i:c:p:121-134.

Ericsson, K. A., Krampe, R. T., & Tesch-Römer, C. (1993). The role of deliberate practice in the acquisition of expert performance. *Psychological Review, 100*, 363-406.

Evolved Analytics LLC. (2021). *DataModeler, Version 9.5.*

Gobet, F. R. (2016). *Understanding expertise: A multidisciplinary approach.* Palgrave.

Nadini, M., Alessandretti, L., Di Giacinto, F., Martino, M., Aiello, L.M., & Baronchelli, A. (2021) Mapping the NFT revolution: market trends, trade networks, and visual features. *Scientific Reports, 11*, 20902. https://doi.org/10.1038/s41598-021-00053-8

Peters, K. (July 08, 2021). *Binance Exchange.* Received from https://www.investo pedia.com/terms/b/binance-exchange.asp

Stein, E.W. (1997). A look at expertise from a social perspective. In P.J. Feltovich, K.M. Ford, & R.R. Hoffman (Eds.), *Expertise in Context: Human and Machine* (pp. 181–194). MIT Press.

Venegas, P. (2021). Trustable risk scoring for non-bank gateways in blockchain and DLT financial networks. In D. Braha, M.A.M. de Aguiar, C. Gershenson, A.J. Morales, L. Kaufman, E.N. Naumova, A.A. Minai, & Y. Bar-Yam (Eds.). *Unifying Themes in Complex Systems X* (pp. 165-178). ICCS 2020.

Wolfram Research, Inc. (2021). *Mathematica, Version 12.2.0*

Journal on Policy and Complex Systems • Volume 7, Number 2 • Fall 2021

Modelling & Simulation of a Rivet Shaving Process for the Protection of the Aerospace Industry against Cyber-threats

Martin Praddaude, Nicolas Hogrel, Matthieu Gay, Ulrike Baumann, Adrien Bécue

Airbus CyberSecurity SAS Metapole 1,
bouvelard Jean Moulin CS 40001 - 78996
Elancourt Cedex France
E-mail: martin.praddaude@airbus.com

Abstract

This paper provides insights on simulation and modelling work performed within CyberFactory#1 project which aims at enhancing optimization and resilience of the Factory of the Future. The paper describes the modelling and simulation of a complete industrial process of rivet shaving, in support to the digitization of aerospace manufacturing. It provides evidence of accurate elaboration of a Digital Twin (DT) of the Roboshave system in the Airbus CyberRange (CR) environment. This work contributes to science and technology by demonstrating the feasibility of a holistic DT of a complex Cyber-Physical System(CPS) throughout its operational and informational layers, including multiple heterogeneous industrial communication protocols. It contributes to industry and practice by providing a highly realistic virtual environment for cybersecurity testing, simulation, training and decision support to enforce security of digitized industrial systems.

Keywords: Simulation, modelling, Cyber-Physical System (CPS), Operational Technology (OT), Industry 4.0, CyberRange (CR), Digital Twin (DT), Programmable Logic Controller (PLC), Industrial Internet of Things (IIoT)

doi: 10.18278/jpcs.7.2.3

Modelado y Simulación de un Proceso de Afeitado de Remaches para la Protección de la Industria Aeroespacial Contra Amenazas Cibernéticas

Resumen

Este documento proporciona información sobre el trabajo de simulación y modelado realizado dentro del proyecto CyberFactory#1, que tiene como objetivo mejorar la optimización y la resiliencia de la Fábrica del Futuro. El artículo describe el modelado y la simulación de un proceso industrial completo de afeitado de remaches, como apoyo a la digitalización de la fabricación aeroespacial. Proporciona evidencia de la elaboración precisa de un Gemelo Digital (DT) del sistema Roboshave en el entorno Cyber Range (CR) de Airbus. Este trabajo contribuye a la ciencia y la tecnología al demostrar la viabilidad de un DT holístico de un Sistema Ciberfísico (CPS) complejo en todas sus capas operativas e informativas, incluidos múltiples protocolos de comunicación industrial heterogéneos. Contribuye a la industria y la práctica al proporcionar un entorno virtual altamente realista para pruebas de ciberseguridad, simulación, capacitación y soporte de decisiones para hacer cumplir la seguridad de los sistemas industriales digitalizados.

Palabras Clave: Simulación, modelado, sistema ciberfísico (CPS), tecnología operativa (OT), industria 4.0, rango cibernético (CR), gemelo digital (DT), controlador lógico programable (PLC), Internet industrial de las cosas (IIoT)

保护太空产业不受网络威胁的铆钉打磨过程建模和模拟

摘要

本文为CyberFactory#1项目执行的模拟和建模工作提供见解，该项目旨在提升未来工厂（Factory of the Future）的优化和复原力。本文描述了完整的工业铆钉打磨过程的建模和模拟，以支持航空制造的数字化。本文提供证据，精确阐述了空客网络靶场（CR）环境中的Roboshave系统数字孪生（DT）。通过证明复杂信息物理系统（CPS）的全面数字孪生在其操作层面和信息层面（包括多个异质工业通信协议）的可行性，本文为科学和技术作贡献。通过提供一个高度现实的虚拟环境，用于网络安全检测、模拟、训练和决策支持，以期执行数字工业系统安全，本文为工业和实践作贡献。

关键词：模拟，建模，信息物理系统（CPS），操作技术（OT），工业4.0，网络靶场（CR），数字孪生（DT），可编程逻辑控制器（PLC），工业物联网（IIoT）

Introduction

CyberFactory#1 project aims at designing, developing, integrating and demonstrating a set of key enabling capabilities to foster optimization and resilience of the Factories of the Future (FoF) (CyberFactory#1-ProjectWeb Page,2019-2022). The project outputs form a totalof12 key capabilities arranged in 3 capacity Layers:

1) Modelling and simulation;

2) Factory of the Future optimization;

3) Factory of the Future resilience.

In this paper we introduce the developments made on the Airbus CyberRange (Airbus CyberSecurity, 2021) for the modelling and simulation of a Cyber-Physical System(CPS) called Roboshave (Bécue et al., 2020), which shaves the rivets of aircraft rudders to keep them within tolerances for airworthiness and aerodynamics (Sterkenburg & Wang, 2021).

Robos have, initially a disconnected equipment, will be connected to a distributed Industrial Internet of Things (IIoT) platform (Sisinni et al., 2018) meant to support real-time monitoring (Chen, 2020), process optimization (Stefano et al., 2020) and quality control (Dutta et al., 2021) in the frame of CyberFactory#1.

In order to specify, test and verify the security and safety properties of the newly connected equipment (Abdo et al., 2018), Airbus CyberSecurity has realized a Digital Twin (DT) (Tao et al., 2019) of the Roboshave system, including simulation of a robotic arm, a profilometer, two Programmable Logic Controllers (PLCs), and Human Machine Interface (HMI). It is integrated in a virtual network environment which accurately replicates the Operational Technology (OT)network (Zhou et al., 2018), the IIoT platform and the Machine Execution System (MES). It features no less than 4 different types of industrial protocols in use within the legacy and newly added communication layers. This development helps solving acknowledged limitations of state of the art DT technology (Tao, Zhang, &Liu, 2019) (Bécue et al., 2020) and provides a demonstration of the effective combination of DT with CR for the purpose of securing Industry 4.0 (Bécue et al., 2018).

Eventually, this digital twin supports the performance of a large panel of attacks, and the definition of adequate security measures based on simulation (Bécue et al., 2018). With the Airbus OT CyberRange, complex industrial automation like Roboshave can be designed, upgraded and tested without any negative impact on the real assets. If maintained in operation, it will also support decision making, both for problems related to manufacturing efficacy or in reaction to new unexpected cyber-threats (Tao et al., 2018).

Methodology

Project Methodology

The project adopts an overall V cycle design methodology (Auriol et al., 2012) in which subcycles corresponding to each of the12 key capabilities are designed in a model-based approach by the use of DTs (Tao et al., 2018). The V cycle is performed through a sequence of work-packages with interactive stages and final deliveries corresponding to output-input transmission: WP2 Requirements and Architecture, WP3 Simulation Capabilities Development, WP4 Optimization Capabilities Development, WP5 Resilience Capabilities Development, WP6 Integration, Validation and Demonstration (ITEA, 2019-2022). The activities described in this paper belong to WP3 and the system simulation will support model-based design and development of subsequent key capabilities, namely the secure deployment of a Data Lake Exploitation capability (Miloslavskaya &

Tolstoy, 2016) in scope of WP4 and the enforcement of Cyber-resilience Mechanisms scope of WP5. Eventually, it will also support hybrid (simulation-based / in operation) validation and demonstration activities in scope of WP6.

Simulation Methodology

The aim is to create a "DigitalTwin." For the simulation, it is possible to separate the different components according to Purdue Reference Model (Williams, 1994):

- On the one hand, level3 and 4 with applications such as kepware/thingworx and ERP

- On the other hand, the lower levels which correspond to the factory floor.

For levels 3 and 4, there is no particular difficulty in creating a simulation, as these are applications running on IT systems. For the levels corresponding to industrial processes, it is more difficult (Thomas, 1999), but it is becoming possible, in particular because the OT and the IT networks use protocols which are more and more similar (Tian & Hu, 2019): ethernet, TCP/IP, and the different providers create simulators for their tools.

In the following, we will indicate the method used to create a shop-floor simulation.

First, it is necessary to define more precisely what we mean by a Digital Twin (Bitton et al., 2018):

- The aim is to be able to simulate cyber-attacks and to have a similar behaviour in the simulated environment as in the real environment (Giuliano & Formicola, 2019),

- This requires the same communications between the simulated equipment as in reality (Su et al., 2017),

- For this, it is necessary to have a virtualization of the different equipment present in the real world,

- In order to be as close to reality as possible, the same projects are used in the automatons; for this, it is often necessary to use the simulators provided by the manufacturers (Negahban & Smith, 2014),

- Yet it is important to notice that vendor DTs commonly are closed proprietary technology, difficult to integrate into a full-model of over-arching industrial process (Bécue et al., 2020).

In order to create the simulation as defined above, we have followed 4 steps:

- Step 1, characteristics of physical assets. The objective of this stage is to recover real equipment:

  - Processor, CPU, RAM, ROM,

  - Features, provider, software, and project

  - Communication with other assets, protocol

- Step 2, find a simulator for each asset. The objective of this stage is to find how it is possible to simulate the asset and the simulator capabilities to communicate:

  - Does the provider have a simulator? If yes, can it communicate with other simulators?

  - Does it use the same protocol as the shop floor? It is also necessary to ascertain the subject of the available licenses.

  - If no simulator is available, it must be determined how to develop one, with the goal to have the same communications.

- Step 3, find out how to simulate the physical process: with a Virtual Machine (VM)? With software? Directly with a simulator?

- Step 4, development of different virtual machines and software defined previously and make them communicate.

Use-Case Description

Airbus Defence and Space owns several sites in Spain which are dedicated to the production and the final assembly line of commercial and military aircrafts (Airbus in Spain, 2021). One of them, Tablada PreFal, next to Seville city centre, is a multi-program, multi-product, and multi-customer plant where Airbus carries out the production of main component assemblies for A400M (Airbus, Airbus A400M,2021), A330MRTT (Airbus A330MRTT, 2021), Boeing 737 (Boeing 737, 2021), C295 (Airbus C295, 2021), CN235 (Airbus C295, 2021), Eurofighter (Airbus Eurofighter, 2021), Falcon 8X (Dassault Falcon 8X, 2021) and A380 (Airbus A380, 2021). Parts of Ariane 6 spacecraft (Airbus Ariane 6, 2021) have begun to be manufactured in 2019. Tablada is modernized and updated constantly in order to be an example to follow in continuous improvement and Industry 4.0. There is a dedicated innovation ecosystem in Tablada facilities for R&D industrial means.

The RoboShave system has been implemented into the Boeing 737 (Boeing 737, 2021) rudder assembly area. A rudder is composed of multiple parts joined together with rivets. The rivets have to be as flat as possible and to re- main within tolerances specified in the requirements (Sterkenburg & Wang, 2021). For that, each rivet is manually shaved to give the rudder the essential aerodynamic characteristics required by such an aircraft part. This impractical operation performed by an operator is very time consuming and slows down the complete production line (Sarh et al., 2009). Following its sense of innovation, Tablada PreFal benefits from the RoboShave system, which has been designed to fulfil an ambitious objective: automate a tedious work with tight tolerances inside a high-rate production line.

Figure 1. RoboShave system overview.

The RoboShave system could be described as a robotic arm whose role is to shave rudder rivets and to automatically check that the shaving operation has been performed successfully. At first, the RoboShave identifies the orientation of the rivet, then the rivet is shaved and to finish the RoboShave checks that the rivet remains inside the tolerances.

This system is planned to be connected with a cooperative network from which the work orders are sent. The data produced by the RoboShave system will be collected in a data lake (Miloslavskaya Tolstoy, 2016) for the purpose of process monitoring, optimization and control (Qin, 2012). The deployment of an IIoT platform extends the attack surface (Sisinni et al.,2018) but this data collection with the deployment of the appropriate technologies based on Artificial Intelligence and Security Incident and Event Monitoring tools will allow to implement predictive

maintenance (Lee et al., 2019) techniques, and detect intrusions to secure
the production level.

Figure 2. First step, the RoboShave identifies the rivet.

Cyber-Range Tool Description

Airbus CyberRange is an advanced simulation platform
that can be used to model IT /
OT systems composed of tens or hundreds of machines and play realistic
scenarios including real cyber-attacks.
The platform manages several environments, isolated ones from the others,
as well as from the legacy IT / OT from
the organization (Airbus CyberSecurity, 2021). By means of these capabilities, users can immerse themselves in
an environment customized to look like
their system in operation. This supports
several use cases including operational qualification, testing, and training
(Bécue et al., 2018). For the hardware,
the tool exists in 2 main forms:

- Physical platform: High performance servers stored in a mobile
  box, on site, switches, hosting VM-
  ware, vSphere Infrastructure.

- Cloud Platform: the CyberRange
  platform is also available in the
Cloud, allowing a flexible and mul-
tisite collaborative experience.

To use the hardware, Airbus CyberSecurity has developed the software
LADE (Life And Death Engine): set of
web and micro services simplifying the
deployment of virtualized infrastructures, running cyber-attacks, tests and
scenarios. LADE allows hybrid infrastructures management. This management software significantly reduces the
delay between designing the simulation
and having it deployed.

The CyberRange offers independent work zones, which represents a
virtual environment dedicated to a user
or a group of users. As a fully custom-
izable platform, the Airbus CyberRange
graphical user interface allows users to
customize their working environment,
add notes and key command lines to
help them pursue exercises (Airbus
CyberSecurity,2021). Each work zone
is totally isolated from the other work
zones, so the actions of one participant
do not interfere with the other partic-

ipants working on other work zones. Each work zone can accommodate standalone replicas of a network architecture or information systems. Interconnecting work zones is possible by connecting a firewall or router in each zone to a shared zone. For further information, reference is made to the Airbus CyberSecurity website (Airbus CyberSecurity, 2021).

Roboshave Process Simulation

To achieve the DigitalTwin associated with the Roboshave system, it is first necessary to establish an overall state of the art of the technology involved. First, we learn about the industrial process in all its layers: asset, integration, communication, information, functional, and business layers, as defined in the Reference Architecture Model for Industry 4.0 (Zezulka et al., 2016). To do this, we establish communication with plant management which will be maintained over time. System information is acquired in formal (writ-

ten documentation) or in formal manners (Stone& Sawyer, 2006). The experience feedback accessible through direct involvement of Roboshave operators is a very important data source in order to obtain all the process subtleties. In addition, it enables the verification of the validity and value of the Digital Twin at any time during construction by having it tested and adopted by manufacturing practitioners (Bärring et al., 2020). With this procedure, we identify the list of physical assets present in the system which need to be included in the scope of simulation. In the case of Roboshave, this scope includes a robotic arm Robot FANUC M-20iA/35M (FANUC M2000 Series, 2021), a profilometer Gocator2120 (LMI3D GOCATOR, 2021), a safety PLC Sick Flexi Soft (SICK Flexi-Soft, 2021), a PLC Siemens S7-1500 (SIEMENS Simatic S7-1500, 2021), and an HMI Siemens TP1500-Comfort (SIEMENS Simatic HMI, 2021). The Physical System in scope of the simulation is called Physical Twin (PT). It is described in Figure 3.

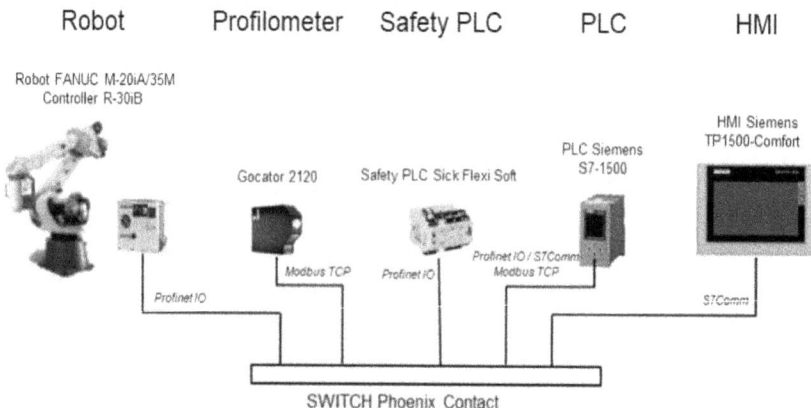

Figure 3. Roboshave System Physical Twin.

We make sure to gather as much information as possible about the constituting elements: equipment manufacturer, product version, technical characteristics, operation modes, hardware and software, connectivity, etc. (Rodič, 2017). In addition, we recover the endemic parts to Roboshave, such as the PLC and HMI projects, but also the various descriptions on the functionalities of the process. We expect to obtain the description of the operations that can be used subsequently in cybersecurity scenarios, such as the different nominal / degraded modes, the segregation of roles in the management of the process, or the expected behaviors of the system depending on the moment (Lou, Guo, Gao, Waedt, & Parekh, 2019). We are also looking for information related to interactions between different assets (Bao, Guo, Li, & Zhang, 2019). Once the industrial system has been understood in depth, the Digital Twin can be built. The DT of Roboshave system, reproducing all elements of its Physical-Twin (TW) is described in Figure 4.

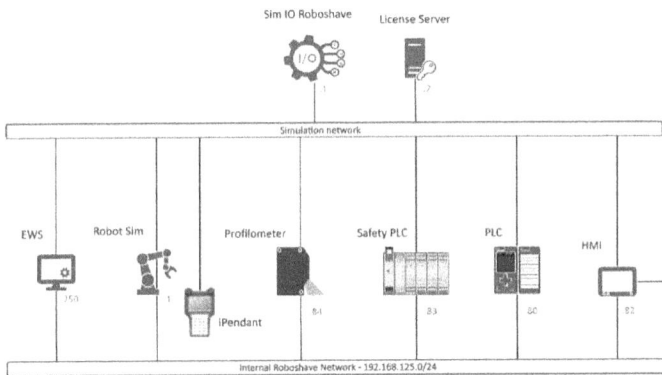

Figure 4. Roboshave System Digital Twin.

For this realization, we relied on the CyberRange virtualization platform from Airbus CyberSecurity (Airbus CyberSecurity, 2021). The tool offers many features to achieve the main objective, such as the ability to build virtual machines on demand, or to perform inter-machine communications. However, certain limitations such as the only Ethernet support as a means of data transmission, or the use of virtualization servers based on x86 processor architectures, will require adaptations to make the Digital Twin functional in this particular context. Indeed, in the industrial world, we can find PLCs operating on particular architectures such as Advanced RISC (Reduced Instruction Set Computing) Machines (ARM) with real-time functionalities (Murti, Jati, Mawardi, & Agustina, 2014).Also industrial systems are commonly interconnected by means of field buses, or even simply with power cables (Kolla, Border, & Mayer, 2003).

In the case where the asset has characteristics that are incompatible with Digital Twin environment constraints, there are three possibilities, listed in decreasing order of application preference:

1. The Digital Twin (DT) environment adapts to the reality of the Physical Twin (PT). In this case, in-depth work is undertaken, often very long and expensive, to align the simulation tool on the characteristics of the PT. In our example, the potential changes of the DT from x86 to ARM, or from Ethernet to a field bus would require the acquisition of new compatible equipment, which had little business relevance.

2. The PhysicalTwin (PT) adapts to the constraints of the Digital Twin (DT) platform. This option should be chosen only if the technology in use suffers from already acknowledged obsolescence or limitations which we aim to overcome. In most cases, it is a costly option that may require a requalification of the manufacturing system. In our example, the potential changes of the PT from ARM to x86, or from field bus to Ethernet would require a requalification of the Roboshave System, which is prohibitive in terms of cost and delay.

3. In some cases, where DT and PT cannot fully align because of particular constraints, the best compromise should be found between the functionalities retained and those to be withdrawn. This compromise should be made according to the considered use and misuse cases. In our example, we want our Digital Twin to operate in x86 architecture, communicating exclusively over Ethernet, but behave in the same way from a functional point of view as the legacy ARM system. With this limitation, we acknowledge that attacks on process variables will be effective, but attacks related to the real-time answers of the system cannot be tested.

4. In this search for adaptation, it is necessary to undertake in-depth search of simulation solutions related to the industrial processing assets. The various criteria are the measured rate of realism, the possible level of exploitation within the virtualization platform, and the time/cost constraints that the solution induces (Hlupic & Paul, 1999). We noticed that the simulation market was more and more expanded, and it had started to affect manufacturers in a concrete way. Indeed, an effective line of research for the construction of a Digital Twin is the use of products from the initial equipment manufacturer (Cabral, Wenger, & Zoitl, 2018). We can compare these solutions to custom-made development of our own simulators in the form of a two entries table to highlight the advantages and disadvantages of vendor-made solutions (Buy) against tailor-made solutions (Make). Such a comparative table is summarized in Table 1.

In Roboshave, most components have existing simulators offered by original equipment manufacturer. RoboGuide software from Fanuc (FANUC Roboguide, 2021) can be used to simulate the robotic arm. GoEmulator from LMI3D (LMI3D Virtual 3D Smart Sensor, 2021) can be used to simulate the profilometer. PLC SimAdvanced (SIEMENS S7PLC SimAdvanced,2021) can be used for PLC simulation. The HMI can be simulated by WinCC software (SIEMENS, SIEMENS WinCC, 2021). Using the original equipment simulator provides a guarantee of quality and time saved, because it theoretically behaves exactly like the physical asset (Post, Groen, & Klaseboer, 2017).

However, some of these simulators suffer from compatibility limitations or constrainful license terms, which limit the range of investigations with consideration for security testing.

In order to overcome these issues, we had to be in close collaboration with providers to solve them. Also despite this evolution in the industrial landscape, we have noticed that there are many devices that do not have their Digital Twin equivalent, especially brands that have never had the need to enter this market. We then proceeded as follows: first of all, we our intentions to the equipment manufacturer, sharing interest in the opportunity to enter the simulation market. Depending on manufacturer willingness and conditions, we may or may not work in collaboration. Table 1 provides a summary of Make / Buy choices, where the selected solution is marked.

Table 1. *Compared Simulations*

Asset	Solution 1 (Buy)	Solution 2 (Make)
Robot Sim	RoboGuide from Fanuc ✓ -Limited connectivity	RoboDK +Free to use
Profilometer	GoEmulator from LMI -Software limitation	Airbus CyberSecurity simulator +Linux compatible ✓
Safety PLC	PLCSimAdv from Siemens -Software limitations	Airbus CyberSecurity simulator +development ✓
PLC	PLCSimAdv from Siemens +Good Compatibility ✓	Airbus Cybersecurity simulator -Limited Fidelity
HMI	WinCC from Siemens +Good Compatibility ✓	Open HMI -Limited Fidelity

Apart from intrinsic component processes, system connectivity also needs comprehensive simulation. Some important links that have been modelled are:

- the S7Comm link between PLCSimAdv (PLC) and WinCC (HMI) to exchange process data

- the S7Comm link between WinCC(HMI) and EWS to load Siemens project

- the S7Comm link between PLCSimAdv (PLC) and EWS to load Siemens project

- the Modbus TCP link between PLCSimAdv (PLC) and Airbus CyberSecurity simulator (Profilometer)

- the Profinet link between PLC and Robot/Safety PLC

It is important to notice that several protocols in use within this list are not supported by the vendor solution.

This is how the development of our own Profinet simulation stack was launched. Profinet is an industrial standard for data communication over Ethernet, designed for collecting data from, and controlling equipment under tight time constraints. The support of this protocol was not yet available during the assembly of this Digital Twin, it is important in Roboshave and is reusable in many other industrial systems (Dias, Sestito, Turcato, & Brandão, 2018). Therefore, we had to undertake extensive research into the operation of this protocol, with the help of the specifications, in order to integrate it technically. This work resulted in a system allowing to capture the communicating devices in Profinet on a network, and to establish a relation between the subsystems. This implementation is represented in Figure 5.

The Profinet layer developed by Airbus CyberSecurity supports certain functionalities resulting from the specifications indicated in IEC61158-5-10 (IEC-International Electrotechnical Commission, 2014) & IEC 61158-6-10 (IEC-InternationalElectrotechnical-Commission, 2019), and can be associated with industrial data processing software such as virtual PLCs, or virtual HMIs. In addition, micro-developments had to be done for various purposes, in particular for the exploitation of the various APIs offered by the manufacturers of simulation software. These have made it possible to change certain variables which are supposed to be modified only by physical behavior (movements, sensors, actuators).

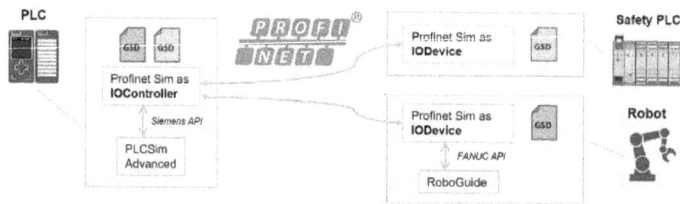

Figure 5. Profinet Simulator Concept.

On Roboshave, we can find different networks with various objectives. These are simulated through virtual networks. However, the program displaying the evolution of the robotic arm in 3D does not necessarily support the possibility of integrating presence sensors which send well-formatted data as expected by the central PLC. In addition, it is normally electrical impulses that are expected. Consequently, it is through an additional simulation network that the robot will send and receive the information to the IO simulator, that a given sensor has changed its state. This network is also used for licensing constraints imposed by manufacturers. As a result, the networks on the real system remain free of noise relating to the simulation (Lu et al., 2020).

Validation Plan

In order to validate the level of fidelity of the digital twin, we carry out a verification phase which uses the physical twin as the model to be achieved. To do this, unit tests are carried out on the simulated machines themselves, as well as according to the capabilities of the complete topology and its interactions. These tests validate the level of the digital twin according to the latter's ability to approximate the behavior of the physical twin. The metrics associated with these tests make it possible to quantify a result. They relate to various aspects: execution time, same behavior between DT and PT with same input conditions, data set exchanged in virtualized network, be-

havior of the assembly according to the technical parameters inserted.

This validation is performed by carrying out a succession of technical and functional tests applied to all aspects of the process. Here are some examples of these tests that can be applied to this use case: Nominal and complete rivet shaving procedure, "Coupon test" procedure, "Open Doors" procedure, Disconnect the Safety PLC and attempt operations known to be dangerous for humans over HMI. Once they have been carried out, this Digital Twin can be used for various purposes: cybersecurity tests, pre-production tests, behavior tests, security tests under specific conditions, industrial log recovery and deployment tests of products adjacent to the initial system etc. (Bécue et al., 2020).

To go further in the digital twin validation process, we can make sure to apply cyber attacks on the latter, which would be replicable on the physical twin. By taking into account the integration constraints, a scope for cyber attacks can be defined to know the limits of the topology. In the event that an attacker reaches Roboshave's internal network, the latter would have the possibility of practicing simple but well-known attacks such as Man-In-The-Middle through ARP (Address Resolution Protocol) Poisoning between OT components, in order to spy on business data (Nam et al., 2012). exchanged, or to cut off the corresponding communications, and thus put the industrial system to an unstable state. The possible consequences of this attack can be loss of the industrial process control by the operator because the link between the HMI and the PLC is cut off, and the data monitored by MES are changed directly from the process in order to raise wrong alarms.

Conclusion and Perspectives

With this work we have demonstrated the feasibility of a holistic simulation of a critical industrial process performed by a complex CPS. It provides advance against state of the art by solving acknowledged limitations of the current technology in terms of simulation framework openness and cosimulation capacity (Bécue et al., 2020). Future work will consist of the diversification of entire cyber scenarios to be developed with punctual attacks in a risk-based approach according to misuse-cases which have been defined and prioritized in previous project works. Further simulation will be integrat-

ed to model other systems included in the IIoT platform such as the Autoclave and the Gap Guns. These DTs will support future design of process optimization and cyber-resilience mechanisms in the frame of CyberFactory#1 (CyberFactory#1-Project Web Page, 2019-2022). An example of a protection mechanism which will be implemented is the deployment of combined user and device access control mechanism compatible with IIoT constraints, based on Airbus CymID solution (Airbus Cybersecurity, 2021). Further security reinforcement mechanisms can be the deployment of OT Itrusion Detection Systems enabling to detect the aforementioned attacks and timely respond (Han, Xie, Chen, & Ling, 2014). In this context, the DT can be used as a decision support tool for response optimization (Bécue, Maia, Feeken, Borchers, & Praca 2020) or as a prediction tool for threat anticipation (Pokhrel, Katta, & Colomo-Palacios, 2020).

References

Abdo, H., Kaouk, M., Flaus, J., & Masse ,F.(2018). A safety/security risk analysis approach of Industrial Control Systems: A cyber bowtie–combining new version of attack tree with bowtie analysis. *Computers & security,72*,175-195.

Auriol, G., Shukla, V., Baron, C., & Fourniols, J.Y. (2012). *Chapter System Engineering Method for System Design*. Intech Open.

Bao, J., Guo, D., Li, J., & Zhang, J.(2019). The modelling and operations for the digital twin in the context of manufacturing. *Enterprise Information Systems, 13(4),* 534-556.

Bärring,M., Johansson,B.,& Shao,G. (2020). DigitalTwin for Smart Manufacturing: The Practitioner's Perspective. *ASME International Mechanical Engineering-*

Congress and Exposition (Vol.84492, p. V02BT02A015). American Society of Mechanical Engineering.

Bécue, A., Fourastier, Y., Praça, I., Savarit, A.,Baron, C., Gradussofs, B., & Thomas, C. (2018). CyberFactory #1—Securing the industry 4.0 with cyber-ranges and digital twins. *2018 14th IEEE International Workshop on Factory Communication Systems (WFCS),*(pp.1-4).

Bécue, A.,Maia, E., Feeken, L., Borchers, P., & Praca, I. (2020). A New Concept of Digital Twin Supporting Optimization and Resilience of Factories of the Future. *Applied Sciences,10(13)*,44-82.

Bitton, R., Gluck, T., Stan, O., Inokuchi, M.,Ohta, Y., Yamada, Y., & Shabtai, A.(2018). Deriving a cost-effective digital twin of an ICS to facilitate security evaluation. *European Symposium on Research in Computer Security*, (pp. 533-535).

Bouzgou, K.& Ahmend-foitih, Z. (2014). Geometric modeling and singularity of 6DOF Fanuc 200IC robot. In Fourth edition of the *International Conference on the Innovative Computing Technology (INTECH 2014)*, (pp.208-214).

Cabral, J., Wenger, M., &Zoitl, A. (2018). Enable co-simulation for industrial automation by an FMU exporter for IEC 61499 models. *IEEE 23rd International-al Conference on Emerging Technologies and Factory Automation (ETFA) (Vol. 1)* (pp.449-455). IEEE.

Chen, W. (2020). Intelligent manufacturing production line data monitoring system for industrial internet of things. *Computer Communications,151*,31-41.

Dias, A. L., Sestito, G. S., Turcato, A.C., & Brandão, D. (2018). Panorama, challenges and opportunities in PROFINET protocol research. *13th IEEE International Conference on Industry Applications (INDUSCON)*(pp.186-193). IEEE.

Dutta, G., Kumar, R., Sindhwani, R., &Singh, R. K. (2021). Digitalization priorities of quality control processes for SMEs: a conceptual study in perspective of Industry 4.0 adoption. *Journal of Intelligent Manufacturing*,1-20.

Giuliano, V., & Formicola, V. (2019). ICSrange: A simulation-based cyber range platform for industrial control systems. *15th European Dependable Computing Conference (EDCC2019)*. eprint arXiv:1909.01910.

Han, S., Xie, M.,Chen, H. H., &Ling, Y. (2014). Intrusion detection in cyber-physical systems: Techniques and challenges. *IEEE systems journal, 8(4)*, pp. 1052-1062.

Hlupic, V., & Paul, R. J. (1999). Guidelines for selection of manufacturing simulation software. *IIE transactions,31(1),*(pp.21-29).

IEC-International Electrotechnical Commission.(2014). *IEC 61158-5-10.*

IEC-International Electrotechnical Commission. (2019). *IEC61158-6-10.*

Kolla, S., Border, D., & Mayer, E.(2003). Fieldbus networks for control system implementations. *Electrical Insulation Conference and Electrical Manufacturing and Coil Winding Technology Conference (Cat.No.03CH37480),* (pp.493-498).

Lee, W.J., Wu, H., Yun, H., Kim, H., Jun, B. M., & Sutherland, J.W. (2019). Predictive maintenance of machine tool systems using artificial intelligence techniques applied to machine condition data. *ProcediaCirp,80,*506-511.

Lou, X., Guo, Y., Gao, Y., Waedt, K.,& Parekh, M.(2019). An idea of using DigitalTwin to perform the functional safety and cybersecurity analysis. *INFORMATIK 2019.* Bonn: Gesellschaft für Informatik e. V.

Lu, Y., Liu, C., Kevin, I., Wang, K., Huang, H., & Xu, X. (2020). DigitalTwin-driven smart manufacturing: Connotation, reference model, applications and research issues. *Robotics and Computer-Integrated Manufacturing,61,101837.*

Miloslavskaya, N., & Tolstoy, A. (2016) Big data, fast data and data lake concepts. *Procedia Computer Science,88,*300-305.

Murti, M.A., Jati, A.N., Mawardi, L., & Agustina, S.A. (2014). Software Architecture of Ladder Compiller to Opcode for Micro PLC Based on ARM Cortex Processor. *Journal of Automation and Control Engineering Vol,2(4).*

Nam, S. Y., Jurayev, S., Kim, S. S., Choi, K., &Choi, G. S. (2012). Mitigating ARP poisoning-based man-in-the-middle attacks in wired or wireless LAN. *EURASIP Journal on Wireless Communications and Networking, 2012(1),*1-17.

Negahban, A., & Smith, J. S. (2014). Simulation for manufacturing system design and operation: Literature review and analysis. *Journal of Manufacturing Systems,33(2),*241-261.

Pokhrel, A., Katta, V., & Colomo-Palacios, R. (2020). DigitalTwin for Cybersecurity Incident Prediction: A Multivocal Literature Review. *IEEE/ACM 42nd International Conference on Software Engineering Workshops* (pp.671-678).

Post, J., Groen, M., & Klaseboer, G. (2017). Physical model based digital twins in manufacturing processes. *10th forming technology forum* (pp.87-92). University of Twente.

Qin, S. J. (2012). Survey on data-driven industrial process monitoring and diagnosis. *Annual review sin control, 36(2),* 220-234.

Rodič, B. (2017). Industry4.0and the new simulation modelling paradigm. *Organizacija,50(3).*

Sarh, B., Buttrick, J., Munk, C., & Bossi, R. (2009). Aircraft manufacturing and assembly. In *Springer handbook of automation* (pp. 893-910). Heidelberg: Springer.

Sisinni, E., Saifullah, A., Han, S., Jennehag, U., & Gidlund, M.(2018). Industrial internet of things: Challenges, opportunities, and directions. *IEEE transactions on industrial informatics,14(11),*4724-4734.

Stefano, F., Benzi, F., & Bassi, E. (2020). IIoT based efficiency optimization in logistics applications. *Asian Journal of BasicScience & Research, 2(4),* 59-73.

Sterkenburg, R., & Wang, P. H .(2021). *Standard aircraft handbook for mechanics and technicians.* McGraw-Hill Education.

Stone, A., & Sawyer, P. (2006). Identifying tacit knowledge-based requirements. *IEE Proceedings-Software, 153(6),*211-218.

Su, W., Antoniou, A., & Eagle, C. (2017). Cybersecurity of industrial communication protocols. *22nd IEEE International Conference on Emerging Technologies and Factory Automation (ETFA)*(pp. 1-4). IEEE.

Tao, F., Qi, Q., Zhang, M., Zhang, H., & Sui, F. (2018). Digital twin-driven product design, manufacturing and servicewith big data. *Int. J. Adv. Manuf. Technol. 2018, 94,* 3563–3576.

Tao, F., Zhang, H., & Liu, A. (2019). Nee, A.Y.C. Digital Twin in Industry: State-of-the-Art. *IEEE Trans. Ind. Inform. 2019,15,* (pp. 2405–2415.).

Thomas, P.J. (1999). *Simulation of industrial processes for control engineers.*Elsevier.

Tian, S., & Hu, Y. (2019). The role of OPC UA TSN in IT and OT convergence. *2019 Chinese Automation Congress (CAC)* (pp.2272-2276). IEEE.

Williams, T. J. (1994). The Purdue enterprise reference architecture.*Computers in industry, 24(2-3),* 141-158.

Zezulka, F., Marcon, P.,Vesely, I., & Sajdl, O. (2016). Industry 4.0–An Introduction in the phenomenon. *IFAC-PapersOnLine, 49(25)*,8-12.

Zhou, L., Zhang, L.,& Ren, L. (2018). Modelling and simulation of logistics service selection in cloud manufacturing. *Procedia CIRP, 72*, 916-921.

Web References

Airbus.(2021, 07 08). *Airbus A330MRTT*. Retrieved from Airbus: https://www.airbus.com/defence/a330mrtt.html

Airbus.(2021, 07 08). *Airbus A380*. Retrieved fromAirbus: https://www.airbus.com/aircraft/passenger-aircraft/a380.html

Airbus.(2021, 07 08). *Airbus A400M*. Retrieved from Airbus: https://www.airbus.com/defence/a400m.html

Airbus.(2021, 07 08). *Airbus Ariane6*. Retrieved from Airbus: https://www.airbus.com/space/launchers-deterrence/ariane-6.html

Airbus.(2021, 07 08). *Airbus C295*. Retrieved from Airbus: https://www.airbus.com/defence/c295.html

Airbus.(2021, 07 08). *Airbus C295*. Retrieved from Airbus: https://www.airbus.com/company/history/defence-history/transport-aircraft.html#C295

Airbus.(2021, 07 08). *Airbus Eurofighter*. Retrieved from Airbus: https://www.airbus.com/defence/eurofighter.html

Airbus.(2021, 07 08). *Airbus in Spain*. Retrieved from Airbus: https://www.airbus.com/company/worldwide-presence/spain.html

Airbus CyberSecurity. (2021, 07 07). *CyberRange*. Retrieved from Airbus Cybersecurity: https://airbus-cyber-security.com/products-and-services/prevent/cyber range/#scroll1

Airbus Cybersecurity. (2021, 09 16). *CymID*. Retrieved from Airbus Cybersecurity:https://airbus-cyber-security.com/wp-content/uploads/2020/12/Airbus-CyberSecurity_CymID_EN.pdf

Boeing. (2021, 07 08). *Boeing 737*. Retrieved fromBoeing: https://www.boeing.com/commercial/737max/

Dassault. (2021, 07 08). *Dassault Falcon 8X*. Retrieved from Dassault Aviation: https://www.dassault-aviation.com/fr/civil/la-famille-falcon/falcon-8x/

FANUC. (2021, 07 12). *FANUC M2000Series*. Retrieved from FANUC: https://www.fanuc.eu/fr/en/robots/robot-filter-page/m-2000-series

FANUC. (2021, 07 12). *FANUC Roboguide*. Retrieved from FANUC: https://www.fanuc.eu/fr/en/robots/accessories/robog uide

ITEA. (2019-2022). *CyberFactory#1-ProjectWeb Page*. Retrieved fromITEA4: https://itea4.org/project/cyberfactory-1.html

LMI3D. (2021, 07 12). *LMI3DGOCATOR*. Retrieved from LMI3D: https://lmi3d.com/brand/gocator-3d-smart-sensors/

LMI3D. (2021, 07 12). *LMI3DVirtual3DSmartSensor*. Retrieved fromLMI3D: https://lmi3d.com/virtual-3d-smart-sensor/

SICK. (2021, 07 12). *SICKFlexi-Soft*. Retrieved from SICK: https://www.sick.com/ag/en/senscontrol-safe-control-solutions/safety-controllers/flexi-soft/c/g186176

SIEMENS. (2021, 07 12). *SIEMENS S7PLC Sim Advanced*. Retrieved from SIEMENS: https://mall.industry.siemens.com/mall/en/WW/Catalog/Products/10316003

SIEMENS. (2021, 07 12). *SIEMENS Simatic HMI*. Retrieved from SIEMENS: https://new.siemens.com/global/en/products/automation/simatic-hmi/panels/comfort-panels.html

SIEMENS. (2021, 07 12). *SIEMENS Simatic S7-1500*. Retrieved from SIEMENS: https://new.siemens.com/global/en/products/automation/systems/industrial/plc/simatic-s7-1500.html

SIEMENS. (2021, 07 12). *SIEMENS WinCC*. Retrieved from SIEMENS: https://new.siemens.com/global/en/products/automation/industry-software/automation-software/scada/simatic-wincc-v7.html

Complex Simulation Workflows in Containerized High-Performance Environment

Vladimr Visnovsky[1]

Viktoria Spisakova[1]

Vojtech Spiwok[2]

Jana Hozzova[1]

Jaroslav Olha[1]

Dalibor Trapl[2]

Lukas Hejtmanek[1]

Ales Krenek[1z]

[1] Institute of Computer Science, Masaryk University, Czech Republic

[2] Department of Biochemistry and Microbiology, University of Chemistry and Technology Prague, Czech Republic

[z] ljocha@ics.muni.cz

Acknowledgements: This work was supported by the Grant Agency of the Czech Republic, grant no. 19-16857S. Computational resources were supplied by the project "e-Infrastruktura CZ" (e-INFRA LM2018140) provided within the program Projects of Large Research, Development and Innovations Infrastructures.

Abstract

Cutting-edge research involving in-silico simulations of-ten requires to use many heterogeneous software tools made by different developers, resulting in complex, custom-made pipelines of various scripts and programs. Such pipelines are nearly impossible to be reproduced by other research groups, jeopardizing both quality and acceptance of such research results.

Starting with two in-house use cases in computational chemistry, we identified a common pattern applicable for other applications as well, and we designed and implemented a solution based on

doi: 10.18278/jpcs.7.2.4

Jupyter notebooks to drive the simulation, Docker containers to package all soft-ware dependencies, and Kubernetes execution environment to run several cooperating containers which build up the whole application.

Keywords: workflow, Jupyter notebook, Docker, Kubernetes, reproducibility, protein folding, molecular force field

Flujos de trabajo de simulación complejos en entornos de alto rendimiento en contenedores

Resumen

La investigación de vanguardia que involucra simulaciones in-silico a menudo requiere el uso de muchas herramientas de software heterogéneas creadas por diferentes desarrolladores, lo que da como resultado canalizaciones complejas y personalizadas de varios scripts y programas. Dichos proyectos son casi imposibles de reproducir por otros grupos de investigación, lo que pone en peligro tanto la calidad como la aceptación de dichos resultados de investigación.

Comenzando con dos casos de uso internos en química computacional, identificamos un patrón común aplicable también para otras aplicaciones, y diseñamos e implementamos una solución basada en portátiles Jupyter para impulsar la simulación, contenedores Docker para empaquetar todas las dependencias de software, y el entorno de ejecución de Kubernetes para ejecutar varios contenedores cooperativos que construyen toda la aplicación.

Palabras Clave: flujo de trabajo, Jupyter notebook, Docker, Kubernetes, reproducibilidad, plegamiento de proteínas, campo de fuerza molecular

容器化高性能环境中的复杂模拟工作流程

摘要

关于in-silico 计算模拟的最新研究经常要求使用许多异质的、由不同开发者设计的软件工具，这造成一系列有关不同脚本和程序的复杂定制系统。这类系统几乎不可能由其他研究团队进行再生产，因此破坏了这类研究结果的质量和接受度。

我们通过计算化学中的两个内部用例，识别了一个适用于其他程序的通用模式，并且我们设计和执行了一个解决方案，该方案基于Jupyter notebooks（驱动模拟），Docker容器（包装所有软件依赖），以及Kubernetes执行环境（驱动建立起整个应用过程的合作容器）。

关键词：工作流程，Jupyter notebook，Docker，Kubernetes，再现性，蛋白质折，分子力场

Introduction

The nature of modern in-silico simulations requires the use of complex pipelines of programs, scripts, and intermediate results. This makes it virtually impossible to reproduce even moderately complex computational experiments for the purpose of validation or extension of existing research.

This known problem is gradually addressed by development of formats and applications such as the Jupyter Notebook (Kluyver et al., 2016) which allow for the exact replication of code pipelines. Container technologies such as Docker (Merkel,2014) can be used to fully package a computing environment, including specific software versions and all of their dependencies, although with growing complexity, the container images become very large and rather difficult to manage.

Besides the issue of reproducibility, another common problem is that complex simulation pipelines tend to have uneven demands on hardware resources, i.e, some parts of the pipeline require much more computational power than others, potentially causing idling and inefficiency during the less intensive parts. A cloud-based service could solve this problem, since it can dynamically allocate more resources for the more intensive parts of the pipeline, and then free the resources for use by other applications; however, the typical overhead associated with spawning or reconfiguring entire virtual machines is rather prohibitive. On the contrary, the Kubernetes platform (Hightower et al., 2017), which provides an environment for running multiple containers and man-aging their mutual interactions, appears to be promising for these purposes.

In this paper, we introduce a deployment setup to address all of these problems. The workflow of the computational experiments is implemented as a Jupyter note-book strictly, which runs in a container with all the necessary lightweight dependencies already pre-installed. The notebook container itself runs in Kubernetes, and it can spawn other jobs (e.g., requesting a node with more CPU cores and RAM temporarily) to run heavyweight dependencies in separate containers. The notebook container itself can be started either by the user manually, or by a simple web front-end application on behalf of the user, bringing additional convenience. The whole setup ensures the reproducibility of the computation (its sequence and software used is controlled strictly), while leveraging the flexibility of resource allocation, as well as making maintenance easier by isolating self-contained software packages in separate containers. We demonstrate a practical usage of the setup on two pilot use cases from computational chemistry.

Related Work

The Binder project (Project Jupyter et al., 2018) addresses the problem of long-term preservation and reproducibility of Jupyter Notebooks. It takes care of storing the versioned notebook in a suitable repository (Git) together with precise information on the environment (base operating system, versioned dependencies etc.). However, it does not handle resource allocation, and it assumes the underlying environment to execute a single Docker container with the notebook.

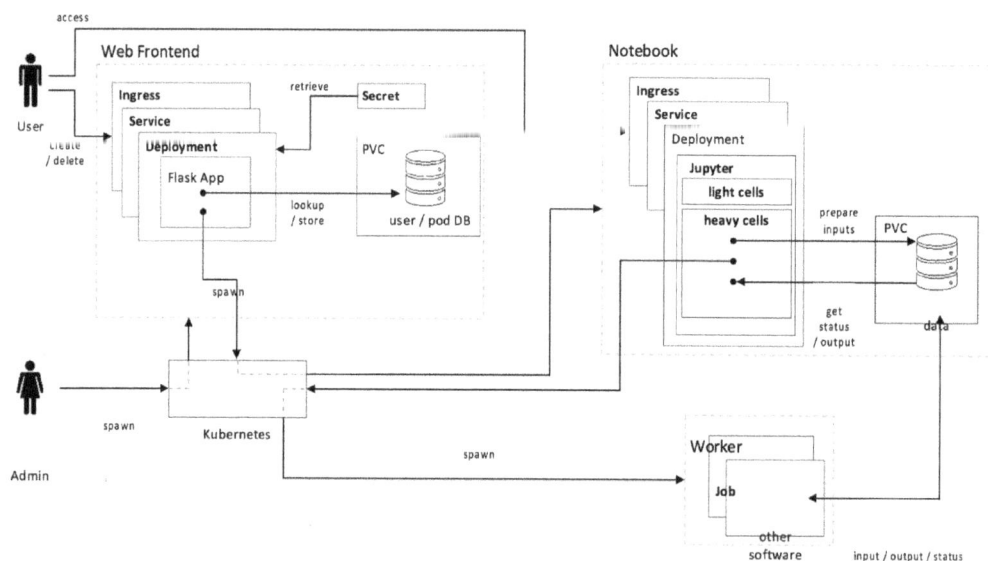

Figure 1. Principal interactions and dataflows among the user, web front end, Kubernetes, notebook and worker containers.

Within the European Open Science Cloud (EOSC) ecosystem, Jupyter Notebooks are one option to access compute resources[1]. The user can specify the required resources, but the allocation is static and it is limited to a

1   https://nootebooks.egi.eu

single container. Recently, the Galaxy project (Afgan et al., 2018) introduced Jupyter Notebook as an interactive environment (Coraor et al., 2021) partially linked to the Galaxy native mechanisms of tracking data provenance. However, the design favors the use of a notebook as a final visualization and analysis step; there are no specific means to control the computation.

Technical Solution

The interactions of all the principal components of the proposed deployment setup are shown in Fig. 1. The application's life starts with the service administrator's action: deploying the application web frontend in Kubernetes and exposing it to the users. The application, implemented in Flask (Grinberg, 2018), performs the following tasks: it authenticates the user, looks up whether there is a running Jupyter notebook belonging to this user, spawns it if not, redirects the user to the notebook endpoint, and deletes the notebook deployment if it is not needed anymore. The frontend is composed of the usual stack of Kubernetes components: Ingress to expose the frontend at a predefined public URL (including a pre-assigned DNS name and a TLS certificate), Service to manage the opened port and to link the Ingress to the deployment, and Deployment which contains the actual Docker container with the frontend application. The mapping between user identities and the running notebooks is maintained in a trivial database which resides in another Kubernetes resource, Persistent Volume Claim (PVC) attached to the Deployment. The choice of user authentication mechanism is arbitrary, just a unique identification of the user is required. We prefer to use the ELIXIR authentication service (Linden et al., 2018).

When the user opens the notebook for the first time, the frontend application deploys a small set of Kubernetes resources forming a functional computational setup. A new PVC is created and attached to the newly-created Deployment to store its working data. The notebook's Ingress resource exposes the notebook on a dynamically assigned DNS name unique for the user. The container starts from an image with the base Jupyter software stack, as well as lightweight dependencies required for the specific application (for example, in our pilot use cases, libraries to read/write chemical le formats and to manipulate molecular structures).

Lightweight computation steps are executed directly in the notebook container. On the other hand, there are steps which require more hardware resources (CPU cores, memory, GPU) and additional complex software stacks (molecular dynamics or quantum chemical simulations in our use cases). We prefer to run these steps in separate containers to allocate the resources only when needed, and to keep more complex pieces of software separate images to streamline their maintenance. The notebook prepares inputs for the heavy computation and stores them on the notebook's PVC. Then, running a heavy cell deploys a Kubernetes Job. It requests the appropriate hardware resources, starts a container from an image containing the necessary software, and mounts the notebook's PVC to access inputs and to store out-puts.

When the user revisits the web frontend again, the application finds the notebook endpoint in its database. If it is still active (different applications may set different notebook lifetimes), the user is redirected there. Otherwise, a new deployment is started and the database is updated. An experienced user can also bypass the web frontend, spawning the payload containers directly.

Pilot Use Cases

Protein folding space exploration

As we reported recently (Krenek et al., 2020), we can use synthetic, artificially generated "landmarks" of a protein to sample the multidimensional landscape of all possible 3D shapes of the protein, and train a neural network model to calculate a non-linear, low-dimensional embedding of this space. Such an embedding can be used to generate a bias potential of the molecule that "pushes" its simulation run in Gro-macs (Abraham et al., 2015) towards not-yet-explored areas of the landscape. Consequently, we can explore biologically interesting behavior of the molecule in significantly shorter simulation time than before.

The main steps of the simulation include the generation of random landmarks, energy minimization, generation of low-dimensional embedding,

neural network training, simulation preparation and execution, and the visualization of results. The minimization, preparation and simulation steps require Gromacs, with the simulation step being the most demanding, taking hours or even days to complete (depending on the molecule). Almost all of the steps (with the exception of NN training and visualization) allow for some level of parallelism; in particular, the main simulation run in Gromacs can be highly parallel, even taking advantage of GPUs.

Table 1 summarizes the main steps of the simulation: the implementation in Jupyter notebook[2] contains more than 50 code cells. Typically, these steps result in visualizations, and the user may tune some of the simulation parameters and repeat certain stages. The table also il-lustrates the heterogeneity of the resource requirements. In this case, we managed to install all but one of the dependencies (Gromacs) in a single container image of rea-sonable size (2.4 GB) which can be built fairly quickly. This is complemented by a dedicated image (400 MB) with Gromacs including extensions for biased sim-ulations (Tribello et al., 2014), where building includes compilation and it runs for up to an hour.

Molecular force field correction

Molecular dynamics simulations rely on so-called force elds, which contain specific parameters that determine the properties of molecules. These parameters are well-tuned for biopolymers

---

2   https://github.com/ljocha/chicken-and-egg/

such as proteins (Lindor-Larsen et al., 2012), but struggle to faithfully reproduce the behavior of smaller organic molecules due to their high chemical diversity. Therefore, the force elds need to be reparametrized for each such molecule.

We provide a pipeline that automatizes this process. It generates landmark structures, and it calculates the correction between accurate quantum mechanics and the less accurate force eld (Trapl et al., 2021). The deployment is available publicly.[3]

Table 2 shows the main steps needed to calculate the molecular force eld correction. Each step is divided into its own set of logically grouped Jupyter notebook cells. Most of these steps can be customized by the user: parameters of calculations can be changed accordingly. Visualizations are provided for the results after multiple steps, and the user can decide whether to change the parameters and repeat the step or continue the computation.

The table also illustrates the needed software. The majority of steps need Gromacs, which uses the same Docker container image as the Protein folding space exploration use case. Another software we need is Orca (Neese et al., 2020), which is containerized in Docker as well (3.4 GB). The rest is installed directly, and no other container is needed.

Conclusions

We identified a common setup pattern in our work on simulations in computational chemistry, and implemented the workflow as a Jupyter Notebook wrapped in a container with all of its dependencies, and running it in Kubernetes. The more demanding steps of the pipeline were isolated in other container images and spawned when needed. The whole solution is interfaced with a simple web front-end. We demonstrated this workflow on two pilot use cases, allowing us to complement our own publications with instant access to completely reproducible implementations of all the experiments. This solution is generic for any applications which follow a similar pattern.

---

3   http://pmcvff-correction.cerit-sc.cz/

Table 1. Essential steps of protein folding simulation. Exact values depend on the simulated protein, short steps are within a few minutes, medium less than an hour, long can take days; medium parallelism can leverage up to 10 cores, high can be dozens (depending on the protein size)

Step	Duration	Parallelism	GPU	Gromacs
Random landmarks	Short	Medium	No	No
Energy minimization	Medium	Medium	No	Yes
Embedding	Short	Medium	No	No
Train NN	Short	No	No	No
Prepare simulation	Medium	Medium	Possible	Yes
Full simulation	Long	High	Yes	Yes
Visualize results	Short	no	no	no

Table 2. Main steps of molecular force eld correction pipeline. Exact values depend on the simulated molecule, short steps take minutes to complete, medium up to an hour, long steps take hours to days.

Step	Duration	Parallelism	GPU	External Software
Molecule visualization	Short	No	No	No
Energy minimization	Medium	No	Possible	Gromacs
Trajectory generation	Medium	Medium	Possible	Gromacs
Configurations clustering	Short	No	No	Gromacs
Train NN	Medium	No	No	No
Energy evaluation	Long	High	No	Orca
Energy minimization	Medium	No	Possible	Gromacs
Visualize results	Short	No	No	No

References

Abraham, M.J., Murtola, T., Schulz, R., Páll, S., Smith, J.C., Hess, B., & Lindahl, E. (2015). GROMACS: High performance molecular simulations through multi-level parallelism from laptops to supercomputers. SoftwareX, 1(2), 19-25. ISSN 2352-7110. doi: 10.1016/j.softx. 2015.06.001.

Coraor, N., Gladman, S., Rasche, H., & Bretaudeau, A. (2021). Galaxy Interactive Tools. Galaxy training. https://training.galaxyproject.org/training-material/topics/admin/tutorials/ interactive-tools/tutorial.html.

Grinberg, M. (2018). Flask web development: developing web applications with python. O'Reilly Media, Inc.

Hightower, K., Burns, B., & Beda, J. (2017). Kubernetes: Up and Running Dive into the Future of Infrastructure (1st. ed.). O'Reilly Media, Inc.

Jalili, V., Afgan, E., Gu, Q., Clements, D., Blankenberg, D., Goecks, J., Taylor, J., & Nekrutenko, A. (2018). The Galaxy platform for accessible, reproducible and collaborative biomedical analyses: 2018 update. Nucleic Acids Research, 46(W1), W537-W544. ISSN 0305-1048. doi:10.1093/nar/gky379.

Kluyver T., Ragan-Kelly, B., Perez, F., & Granger, B. (2016). Jupyter Notebooks-a publishing format for reproducible computational workflows. In F. Loizides & B. Schmidt (Eds), Positioning and Power in Academic Publishing: Players, Agents and Agendas (pp. 87-90). IOS Press.

Krenek A., Hozzova , J., Olha, J., Trapl, D., & Spiwok, V., (2020). Exploring Protein Folding Space with Neural Network Guided Simulations. In MODELLING AND SIMULATION 2020. EUROSIS-ETI. ISBN 978-94-92859-12-9, 305{309.

Linden, M., Prochazka, M., Lappalainen, I., Bucik, D., Vyskocil, P., Kuba, M., Silén, S., Belmann, P., Sczyrba, A., Newhouse, S., Matyska, L., & Nyrönen, T. (2018). Common ELIXIR Service for Researcher Authentication and Authorisation. F1000Research. doi:10.12688/ f1000research.15161.1.

Lindor-Larsen, K., Maragakis, P., Piana, S., Eastwood, M., Dror, R.O., & Shaw, D.E. (2012). Systematic Validation of Protein Force Fields Against Experimental Data. PLoS One, 7(2). doi:10.1371/journal.pone.0032131.

Merkel, D. (2014, May). Docker: Lightweight Linux containers for consistent development and deployment. Linux Journal.

Neese, F, Wennmohs, F., Becker, U., & Riplinger, C. (2020). The ORCA quantum chemistry program package. J Chem Phys, 152(22). doi: 10.1063/5.0004608.

Project Jupyter, Forde, J., Bussonnier, M., & Freeman, J. (2018). Binder 2.0 - Reproducible, Interactive,

Sharable Environments for Science at Scale. Proceedings of the 17th Python in Science Conference, 113-120. doi:10.25080/Majora-4af1f417-011.

Trapl, D., Krupicka, M. Visnovsky,, V., Hozzova , J., Olha, J., Krenek, A., & Spiwok, V. (2021). Property map collective variable as a useful tool for force field correction. J Chem Inf Model. Submitted.

Tribello, G.A., Bonomi, M., Branduardi, D., Camilloni, C., & Bussi, G. (2014). PLUMED 2: New feathers for an old bird. Computer Physics Communications, 185(2), 604-613. DOI:10.1016/j.cpc.2013.09.018.

Augmented Reality Implementation for Comfortable Adaptation of Disabled Personnel to the Production Workplace

Oleg Surnin, Pavel Sitnikov
Open code
55 Yarmarochnaya Samara, Russia
E-mail: sitnikov@o-code.ru

Alexandr Gubinkiy, Alexandr Dorofeev
Samaraavtozhgut 11 Dzerzhinskogo Samara, Russia
E-mail: info@samjgut.com

Tatiana Nikiforova, Arkadiy Krivosheev,
Vladimir Zemtsov, Anton Ivaschenko
Samara State Technical University
244 Molodogvardeyskaya Samara, Russia
E-mail: anton.ivashenko@gmail.com

Acknowledgement: The paper was supported by RFBR, according to the research project № 20-08-00797.

Abstract

The paper presents the results of augmented reality system development and implementation for labour rehabilitation and adaptation of personnel with disabilities at modern manufacturing enterprise. Primary main attention is given to the production quality control using the computer vision system based on an artificial neural network. Simulation is used to produce the mixed reality for partially disabled personnel to provide comfortable adaptation of the production workplace. The research results were deployed and probated at a specialized enterprise that produces automobile cables and wires.

Keywords: smart manufacturing systems, intelligent simulation environments, neural networks, augmented reality, computer vision, rehabilitation

doi: 10.18278/jpcs.7.2.5

Implementación de Realidad Aumentada para la Adaptación Cómoda del Personal con Discapacidad al Puesto de Producción

Resumen

El artículo presenta los resultados del desarrollo e implementación de un sistema de realidad aumentada para la rehabilitación y adaptación laboral del personal con discapacidad en una empresa manufacturera moderna. Se presta especial atención al control de calidad de la producción utilizando el sistema de visión artificial basado en una red neuronal artificial. La simulación se utiliza para producir la realidad mixta para personal parcialmente discapacitado para proporcionar una adaptación cómoda del lugar de trabajo de producción. Los resultados de la investigación se implementaron y probaron en una empresa especializada que produce cables y alambres para automóviles.

Palabras Clave: Sistemas de Fabricación Inteligente, Entornos de Simulación Inteligente, Redes Neuronales, Realidad Aumentada, Visión Artificial, Rehabilitación

通过增强现实让残障人士舒适适应生产工作地点

摘要

针对在现代制造企业工作的残障人士的劳动康复和适应，本文提供了增强现实系统开发和执行的结果。主要聚焦于通过计算机视觉系统（基于人工神经网络）进行的生产质量控制。使用模拟技术为残障人士制造混合现实，以期提供舒适的生产工作地点适应。研究结果在一家专业化的汽车电缆制造企业中加以应用和检验。

关键词：智能制造系统，智能模拟环境，神经网络，增强现实，计算机视觉，康复

Introduction

Modern simulation technologies implemented by the computer vision and augmented reality systems become an efficient facility for rehabilitation of people with disabilities. This subject refers to a vocational counseling, whose goal is to assist and empower individuals with various disabilities to achieve their career goals in the most integrated setting possible. This problem is particularly topical for modern production enterprises that are removing manual operations with robotic devices and artificial intelligence, but that are able to introduce new job opportunities.

In the sphere of labour rehabilitation, information technologies are used to reduce routine and physically taxing work conditions or support the personnel by providing them with additional visual or audio information. However, a complete replacement of humans by robots still remains an inefficient measure. Human staff is more adaptive and reliable to fulfill the casual work or outstanding services. Therefore, efficiency of a modern manufacturing enterprise depends on an optimal balance between the personnel and Artificial Intelligence.

In this paper we present a solution of rational application of Artificial Intelligence in a modern production enterprise, considering an additional parameter of employing the staff with the impairment of visual performance. This additional requirement necessitates a review of the optimization problem of modern enterprise automation to find a solution in the balancing of humans and robots.

State of the Art

Medical rehabilitation (Aramaki, 2019; Cao, 2016; Ivaschenko, 2021; Tieri, 2018) using the full stack of modern information technologies is a growing and promising area of computer science. Labour rehabilitation is comparatively less frequently discussed, but nevertheless an equally important area of scientific research reflected in a number of papers (Bell, 2013; Rehabilitation 2003).

The goal of social and labour rehabilitation is the comfortable adaptation of a disabled person to the workplace in production conditions and the development of an active life position. This problem remains salient for modernized enterprises that actively implement new information technologies. According to the concept of Industry 4.0 (Lasi, 2014), smart manufacturing enterprises reorganize their production processes on the basis of new technologies including robotics, the Internet of Things, Computer Vision, Augmented Reality, etc.

Technologies provide new opportunities for comfortable adaptation to production workplaces, including the improvements required by the personnel with disabilities. In particular, nowadays vision disabilities can be compensated for with modern hardware and software solutions for computer vision and image processing

(Sonka, 2008; Wiley, 2018) supplied with adaptive user interfaces capable of developing the mixed reality.

Related works of modern information technologies implementation of rehabilitation of people with visual disabilities are presented in (Bhandari, 2019; Kumar, 2014; Rajendran, 2020; Suresh, 2019). However, the problem of comfortable adaptation of disabled personnel to the production workplace is more specific and requires additional study.

Considering the requirements of a modern enterprise that employs the personnel with vision disabilities, the intelligent solution is designed to be built on the basis of a combination of artificial neural networks and knowledge bases (ontologies) used for logical reasoning (Egmont-Petersen, 2002; Goodfellow, 2016; Ivaschenko, 2020; Staab, 2009). Such integration allows consolidating the capabilities of pattern recognition and decision-making support for better adaptation of workplaces.

Below we present a new solution to apply Artificial Intelligence in a modern production enterprise considering an additional parameter of employing the staff with the impairment of visual performance.

Problem Statement

The problem of modern digital technologies implementation was stated by a unique production enterprise Samaraautozhgut. It is a producer of wires and accessories for automotive wiring harnesses in Samara region in Russia and employs persons with vision disability. Considering this factor, the systems of computer vision are hardly required at such an enterprise to help disabled employees increase the production efficiency and quality. At the same time the stated problem considers automated help of employees but not removing them by robots.

Typical stages of the production process are illustrated by Fig. 1.

Figure 1. Wire Assembly and Testing Process.

In this context comfortable adaptation of the personnel means supplementing them with additional interactive user interfaces based on sound notifications and Augmented Reality that provide additional information and thus helping them to reduce the errors caused by disability.

To solve this problem there was proposed an original hardware and software solution implementing the modern technologies of computer vision. The expected system features include automatic sorting, defect recognition and quality control. Quality control of products and production processes in turn provides for the implementation of photo / video processing of the results of monitoring e.g., assembly of parts and components, and control of the facts of operations performed.

The module for photo / video control of production processes should be implemented at a high level of usability and take into account all the features, advantages and disadvantages of a particular camera from which the video stream is captured and should be an application that works in full screen mode.

Additionally, the interface of the photo / video control module of production processes should provide for content management – pause / resume, fast forward / rewind, and also provide the ability to switch between several alternative screens for visual display.

The module for controlling the fact of performing operations based on the video stream in real time should recognize and control the steps actually taken in the production process and indicate the mistakes made, thereby correcting the process executor.

In this regard, the computer vision system is intended to:

- recognize the production process of assembling / testing harnesses;

- control the production process of assembly / testing of harnesses;

- inform the contractor about errors made during the assembly / testing of harnesses.

Solution Results

To implement the control of the fact of performing operations, the configuration of a convolutional neural network (CNN) was used. CNN provides image recognition and identifies the objects involved in the production process.

Experimental studies have shown that this is the optimal solution for working in real time, which makes it possible to accurately process the input data from the video stream and perform the assigned tasks.

In order to automate the finding and classification of images, the Tensor Flow framework was used, which is a library for machine learning. The OpenCV computer vision library was used for preliminary image processing. To accelerate the training of the neural network, a server with a GPU was used.

To train the neural network, five classes of recognition objects were defined:

- assembly gun;

- corrugated tube;

- clamp (wire fastening);

- operator assembling the wire;

- hands of the operator performing the assembly.

The first step was to prepare the data. A test video was originally created. The video showed various stages of the wire assembly from different positions and viewing angles (5 assemblies in total, there was only one assembly in the frame). For each class there were 4,000 images of the training dataset (the exception was the class of people: 2,000 images).

Since CNN was chosen as the architecture, further it was necessary to determine:

- dimension of the input image and output layers of the neural network;

- number and dimension of neural network convolution layers;

- number and dimension of down-sampling layers of the neural network.

After that, its markup was carried out, which was necessary for training the neural network. A total of 9,437 images were obtained. The dimension of the training and test images corresponded to the dimension of the CNN input layer. The training of the neural network consisted in optimizing the weight matrixes $W = \{W1, W2,..., Wn-1\}$, where n is the sum of the number of convolutional layers and subsampling layers. Gradient descent and back propagation algorithms were used as learning algorithms for the CNN. During the training, a subset $S' \subset S$ was used.

For this video, a CSV file was created, where at every tenth frame it was noted which recognition object was presented on the screen. The final data were reflected in the table, where the average probability was marked for 5 objects and the final average value of the entire neural network for this set was calculated.

As a result, the CNN consisted of one input image, two convolutional and two down-sampling layers (subsampling layers). The dimensions of the layers and the input image are presented in Table 1.

Layer	Dimension	Feature maps number
Input Image	416x416x3	5
First convolutional layer	208x208x3	5
First layer of subsampling	13x13x1024	5
Second layer of convolution	104x104x64	5
Downsampling layer	13x13x2048	5

Then, by varying the number of epochs and testing the neural network on the test sample, the optimal number of epochs was determined (the minimum number was 25, corresponding to the number of epochs). Ultimately, after 20 000 steps, the probability exceeded 0.93, after which it did not change much (see Fig. 2).

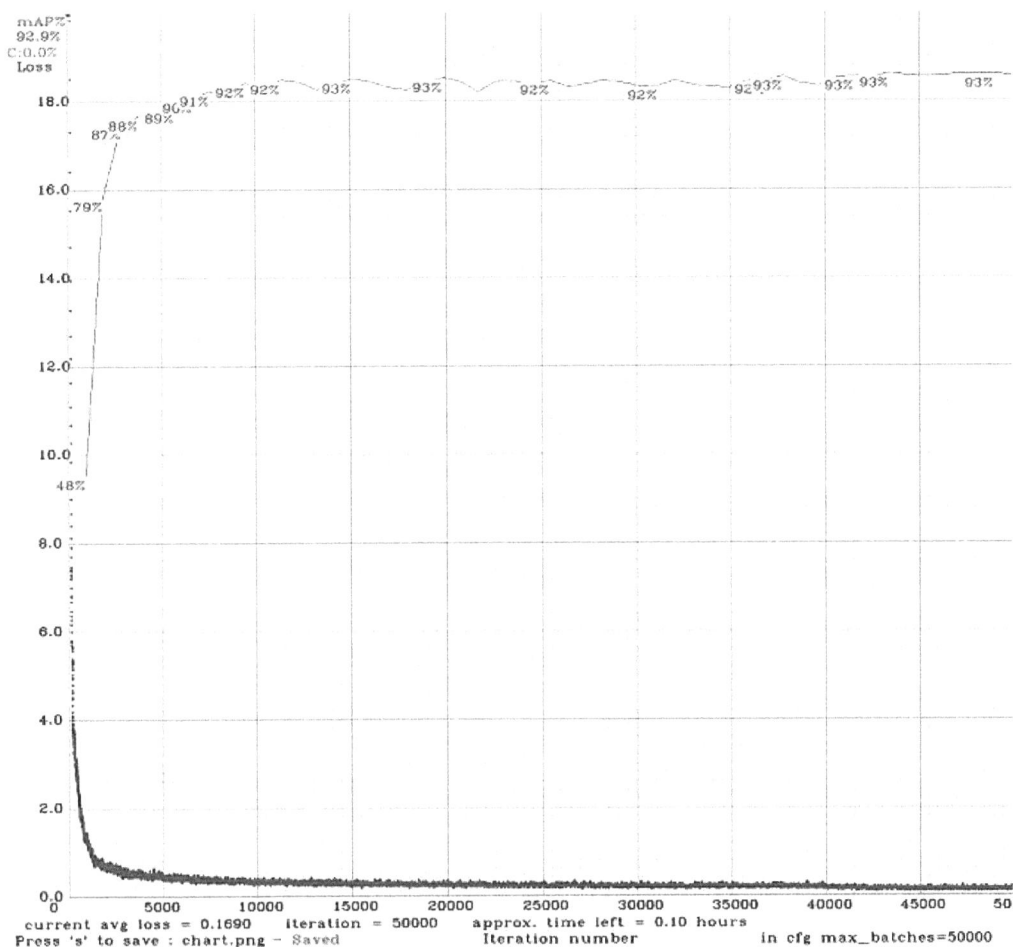

Figure 2. Probability of recognition (red line) and loss function (blue line).

An ontological approach was applied to describe the characteristic information about recognition objects (classes of objects used in the assembly of an automobile harness), as well as information about the production process, including technological operations of assembling and testing the wires in accordance with production and route maps.

The projected knowledge base provides:

- creating, editing, and deleting objects, and attributes;

- creating, editing, and deleting relations between the objects;

- navigation between objects of the subject area based on named relations in the knowledge base;

- description, binding, and implementation of existing rules without restarting the system;

- semantic search and knowledge visualization.

Using the specifically designed software called "Ontology constructor" allows you to add new information to

63

the knowledge base without changing the program code. This feature, implemented in the manual operations control system, allows you to enter information into the knowledge base when making changes to the technological process during the assembly and testing of automobile wires, as well as describe a new production process for assembling and testing.

The generated semantic network accumulates the acquired knowledge of the manual operations control system in the form of recognition objects and links between them. In the future, this knowledge can be used to form logical onclusions and a text description of the operations performed.

Combination of the Ontology and CNN allows selection of image recognition method and setting of intelligent algorithms in accordance with the requirements for a given workplace.

Implementation

The software implements the following main functions:

- recognition of the production process of assembly / testing of wires based on video filming in real time;

- control of the production process of assembly / testing of wires based on video filming in real time;

- informing the contractor about errors made during the assembly / testing of wires;

- saving data about the contractor's mistakes made during the assembly / testing of wires.

To control the assembly and test the wire, you must first create in the system a standard with marked recognition areas for wires of each type (number) to be checked. To do this, in the opened form "Create a wire" on any of the cameras, select a square area with the mouse cursor, and go sequentially to each field for entering data and creating a list of stages and operations of the technological process for the selected wire (see Fig. 3).

The functions performed by the operator allow him to:

- receive informational messages (hints) on the order of the wire assembly;

- receive informational messages about errors made during the build process;

- control modes (control of modes of technological operations);

- manage recognition modes.

The operator assembles the technical product. The system prompts the assembly order, highlighting the structural elements involved in the assembly process, signaling the errors if they occur.

At the next step the system checks the performance of cameras for the presence of a video signal. If a malfunction (lack of signal) is detected from any of the cameras, the system will inform the user with a corresponding message.

Upon successful completion of the camera health check, the System is

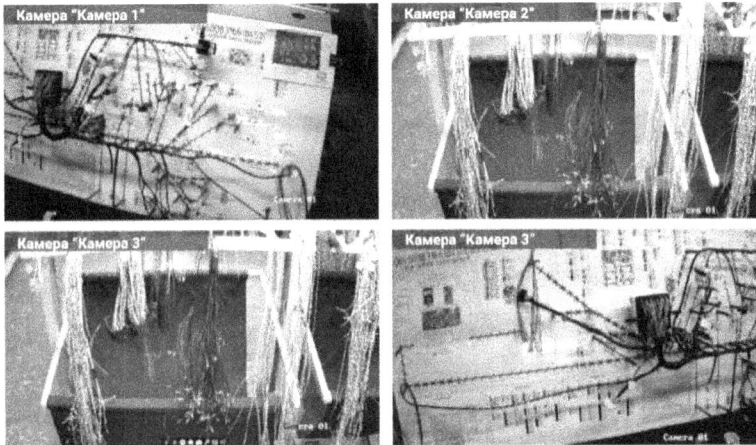

Figure 3. Setup of the wire production process.

Figure 4. Production operation recognition and control in augmented reality.

ready to perform control over the operations. Then the user proceeds to the execution of the stages, according to the production process.

The user at the workplace performs the steps and actions, according to the technological process of assembling and testing the wires, namely:

- installing the wire;

- installation of the elements;

- fastening elements;

- removing the wire.

In case of erroneous actions of the user at any stage of the process, the system displays an informing window about the error he made with sound notification. The system shows at what stage the user skipped a certain action, thereby controlling the production process.

As presented in Fig. 4 the additional notifications are introduced in the form of simulated elements that are visualized above the real ones in a mixed reality scene. Their appearance can be supplemented by corresponding sound alerts.

In the exceptional case when the system incorrectly determines the user's action, it provides the ability to perform visual control instead of automated one. In this case, the user can use the "Skip" button to force confirmation of the operation. Information about its action is reported into the "Defect log" for further analysis.

Therefore, additional visual elements are added to the user interface helping the personnel to overcome the problems caused by the lack of visual information and thus provide comfortable adaptation of the workplace.

Let's consider an example of the functioning of the system using the example of assembling the typical wire. To check the quality of recognition of manual operations and to receive contextual instructions on the assembly order, the wire was assembled with and without making an error: inconsistency of the operation with the route map with the assembly of the automobile harness.

After choosing the harness number and checking the cameras for operability, the harness assembly began. To check the quality of recognition by the system, an error was simulated when performing the stages of installing the harness elements (see Fig. 5).

Information about an error (violation of the wire assembly sequence) appeared on the left side of the screen and on the main screen. In this case, the fact of the error was determined by means of a neural network. At the same time, contextual information about the error and information on actions to eliminate the error and continue the correct assembly of the harness was obtained from the knowledge base of characteristic information.

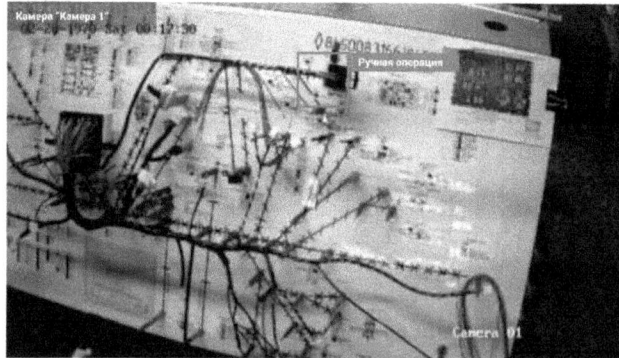

Figure 5. Experimental stand of the dual-fuel engine.

All information about the mistakes made during the assembly of the harness goes to the "Defect log" with the entry of the information into the knowledge base. The "Defect log" window receives information about the errors recorded by the user, made at the stages of assembly and testing, and also contains filter controls for displaying data in a convenient form.

As a result, 20 assemblies (identical technological operations) were carried out. Out of 20 processes carried out, the System in 1 case could not recognize the error. The recognition process exceeded 95%, which indicates a high rate exceeding the probability of an operator making a mistake, without using a manual control system.

Conclusion

Implementation of modern intelligent technologies allows not only reducing the personnel but also providing comfortable adaptation of the production workplace. The proposed solution based on computer vision does not remove the human worker but helps him by identifying and reporting the errors, caused by the disability. Ad-ditionally, it provides instructions on which step in the production process is the next one, i.e., it can support the human worker by reminding him of the general production process.

Therefore, the presented results illustrate the efficiency of quality control at the manufacturing enterprise employing personnel with visual disabilities. Next research steps are concerned with deep study of adaptation of disabled personnel to the production workplace considering the human factor and features of modern technologies of Artificial Intelligence.

References

Aramaki, A.L., Sampaio, R.F., Reis, A.C.S., Cavalcanti, A., & Silva e Dutra, F.C.M. (2019). Virtual reality in the rehabilitation of patients with stroke: an integrative review. *Arquivos de Neuro-Psiquiatria, 77*(4), 268-278.

Bell, E., & N. Mino. (2013). Blind and visually impaired adult rehabilitation and employment survey: final results. *Journal of Blindness Innovation and Research, 3*(1). http://dx.doi.org/10.5241/2F1-35

Bhandari, A., Prasad, P.W.C., Alsadoon, A., & Maag, A. (2019). Object detection and recognition: Using deep learning to assist the visually impaired. *Disability and Rehabilitation: Assistive Technology, 16*, 1-9. 10.1080/17483107.2019.1673834.

Cao, S. (2016). Virtual reality applications in rehabilitation. In M. Kurosu (Ed.) *Human-Computer Interaction. Theory, Design, Development and Practice. HCI 2016. Lecture Notes in Computer Science*, Volume 9731 (pp. 3-10). Springer.

Egmont-Petersen, M., de Ridder, D. & Handels, H. (2002). Image processing with neural networks – a review. *Pattern Recognition, 35* (10), 2279-2301.

Goodfellow, I., Bengio, Y., & Courville, A. (2016). *Deep learning, vol. 1*. MIT Press.

Ivaschenko, A., Krivosheev, A., & Nikiforova, T. (2020). Pragmatic model for human role definition in mixed intelligence solutions. *Proceedings of the 4th annual science fiction prototyping conference*, 19-23.

Ivaschenko, A., Kolsanov, A., Chaplygin, S. & Rovnov, S. (2021). Hand simulation for VR based rehabilitation. *Proceedings of the 5th Annual Science Fiction Prototyping Conference*, 57-59.

Kumar, A. (2014). Rehabilitation of the blind using audio to visual conversion tool. *Journal of Biomedical Engineering and Medical Imaging, 1*, 24-31. 10.14738/jbemi.14.395.

Lasi, H., Fettke, P., Feld, T., & Hoffmann, M. (2014). Industry 4.0. *Business & Information Systems Engineering, 4*(6), 239-242.

Rajendran, P.S., Krishnan, P., & Aravindhar., D.J. (2020). *Design and implementation of voice assisted smart glasses for visually impaired people using Google Vision API.* 4th International Conference on Electronics, Communication and Aerospace Technology (ICECA), 1221-1224.

Rehabilitation and integration of people with disabilities: policy and legislation (7th edition) (2003). Council of Europe Publishing.

Sonka, M., Hlavac, V., & Boyle, R. (2008). *Image processing, analysis, and machine vision* (3rd edition). Thomson

Staab, S., & Studer, R. (2009). *Handbook on Ontologies* (2nd edition). Springer-Verlag.

Suresh, A., Arora, C., Laha, D., , Gaba, D., & Bhambri, D. (2019). Intelligent smart glass for visually impaired using deep learning machine vision techniques and robot operating system (ROS). *Robot Intelligence Technology and Applications, 5*, 99-112.

Tieri, G., Morone, G., Paolucci, S. & Iosa, M. (2018). Virtual reality in cognitive and motor rehabilitation: Facts, fiction and fallacies. *Expert Review of Medical Devices, 15*(2), 107-117.

Wiley, V., & Lucas, T. (2018). Computer vision and image processing: a paper review. *International*

Designing an Emergency Information System for an Emergency Information System for Catastrophic Natural Situations

K. Papatheodosiou and C. Angeli

School of Engineering
University of West Attica
Ancient Olive Grove Campus
P. Ralli and Thivon
250 Egaleo, Athens, Greece

E-mail: kopa@uniwa.gr
angeli@uniwa.gr
c_angeli@otenet.gr

Abstract

Natural disasters have brought about irreparable damage to humans, human activity, society, and the economy, and their effects will probably be increased in the future due to climate change. However, the extent of a natural disaster could be diminished if both individuals and authorities are informed of an impending emergency situation. Therefore, the research interest has been directed into developing robust Emergency Information Systems. This paper demonstrates the way a specific Emergency Information System could be designed to deliver alert messages. The system was designed on the base of the DRM standards and was put into action in the region of Vigla, an area located in Symi, one of the Dodecanese islands. The coverage test proved that the system operates well in remote areas that are characterized by rough geographic terrain.

Keywords: warning system, emergency, emergency information system

Diseño de un Sistema de Información de Emergencia para Situaciones Naturales Catastróficas

Resumen

Los desastres naturales han provocado daños irreparables a los seres humanos, la actividad humana, la sociedad y la economía, y

doi: 10.18278/jpcs.7.2.5

probablemente su efecto se verá incrementado en el futuro debido al cambio climático. Sin embargo, el alcance de un desastre natural podría disminuir si se informa tanto a las personas como a las autoridades de una situación de emergencia inminente. Por lo tanto, el interés de la investigación se ha dirigido al desarrollo de Sistemas de Información de Emergencia robustos. Sobre esta base, este documento demuestra la forma en que se podría diseñar un Sistema de Información de Emergencia específico para enviar mensajes de alerta. El sistema fue diseñado sobre la base de los estándares DRM y se puso en marcha en la región de Vigla, un área ubicada en Symi, una de las islas del Dodecaneso. La prueba de cobertura demostró que el sistema funciona bien en áreas remotas que se caracterizan por un terreno geográfico accidentado.

Palabras Clave: Sistema de Alerta, Emergencia, Sistema de Información de Emergencia

为自然灾害场景设计应急信息系统

摘要

自然灾害已为人类、人类活动、社会和经济带来了不可修复的破坏，并且由于气候变化，其灾害影响将在未来增加。不过，如果个体和当局能知晓即将到来的紧急情况，气候灾害程度则能减少。因此，研究兴趣聚焦于开发稳健的应急信息系统。基于此，本文证明了一个具体的应急信息系统能如何通过设计来交付预警信息。该系统的设计基于灾害风险管理（DRM）标准，并在锡米岛（多德卡尼斯群岛之一）的Vigla区域中投入使用。覆盖范围检测证明，该系统在偏远区域（崎岖地形）中运行良好。

关键词：警报系统，紧急情况，应急信息系统

Introduction

In recent years, we have been witnessing many natural disasters such as earthquakes, floods and fires that have necessitated the development of Emergency Information Systems, aiming to inform the public and authorities of an impending emergency situation. A critical issue that pops up when tackling such disasters is the loss of communication systems. However, such loss could be counterbalanced by a competent emergency information system which could be available and well operated in case of emergency.

The technology which could be employed in order to develop an Emergency Information System should compensate for the system stability in the case of a disaster. Various technologies could be used for this purpose. Tarchi et al. (2009) have presented an emergency information system which incorporates the mobile network model into the communication infrastructure. Bai et al. (2010) has proposed an integrated communication system that consists of heterogeneous wireless networks pointing upward; in the case of remote areas, a satellite gate is needed to achieve the connection with the satellite mobile network. Lien et al. (2009) have demonstrated an emergency information system based on ad-hoc networks (MANET). Choi & Lee (2008) point out that satellite communication networks are considered to be the best solution to the radio broadcasting of the emergency content. Bartel et al., (2009) suggest that an emergency information system should be a part of an integrated information system (EMIS), which incorporates dynamic GIS databases, so that the emergency information could be processed and transmitted in real time.

However, Kang & Choo (2016) state that Emergency Information Systems based on the capabilities of cellular phones, emails, and text messaging services cannot send the requisite alert message to all individuals, nor are they effective for a location-oriented emer-

gency. Proloy et al. (2017) direct attention to the need for secure and reliable transmission through wireless networks, laying stress on the use of modulation techniques to combat the bits error. Forstmann et al. (2011) argue that networks such as Ethernet and WIFI will be susceptible to failure in times of emergency, especially in the case where the electrical power goes out.

Another issue is related to the quality of the emergency information provided. Endsley et al. (2011) and Jennex (2007) argue that emergency information should be provided rapidly and accurately. In addition, Endsley, Bolte, & Jones (2011) and Jennex (2007) suggest that emergency information should be provided immediately after the onset of the emergency.

A further important issue focuses on the extent of the availability of the technologies that could be used to develop an Emergency Information System in remote areas. Jang et al. (2009) have underlined that a critical issue which arises when coping with disasters is the loss of communication systems. It is important to emphasize that technologies such as the internet and wireless networks are not always available in remote areas. This holds true especially in the case of remote islands. In spite of the fact that some remote areas are served through such technological facilities, the service provided frequently lacks quality and therefore it is not feasible for an Emergency Information System developer to use such a service. In such cases, other potential technologies such as Digital Radio Broadcasting, Digital Television, and GIS systems could offer more efficiency to the final emergency information system

This paper takes up the issue of emergency information system development by focusing attention on the technologies that could be employed, laying stress on DRM technology (Section 2). The paper also demonstrates a competent emergency information system which works well in remote areas (Section 3.1). A specific methodology was used to test the coverage potential of our system (Sections 3.2). The system was put into action and the results were promising (Section 3.3) The final Sections 4 and 5 include the discussion on the results and the concluding remarks.

Literature Review

There are a lot of studies related to an Emergency Information System Development that we find in Literature. Kang & Choo (2016) have developed an Emergency Information System for car accidents and natural disasters based on a respective warning system by employing a deep-learning technology. Specifically, an emergency warning system was developed relying on deep-based real time videos on CCTV devices in order to detect car accidents and natural disasters. Also, an Information System was developed in order to inform authorities of an impending car accident or an impending natural disaster.

The study of Siergiejczyk (2015) refers to an Emergency Information System that could be used in railway sta-

tions in order to inform the personnel of impending dangers that could necessitate the stoppage of train movement. This Emergency Information System takes advantage of the GSM-R service capabilities and, at the time a specific danger is being noticed, an alarm signal is being sent to the railway personnel through the use of a voice group call service (VGCS).

The work of Khalid & Shafiai (2015) places emphasis on an Emergency Information System based on a respective warning system for floods in Malaysia. The information delivery process focuses on publishing the information of an impending flood, derived from a corresponding warning system online, so that people could get access to this information. Simultaneously, at the time a flood is being predicted, short text messages (SMS) are being sent to authorities in order to take the requisite action.

The American Patent (2018) suggests using Digital Radio Broadcasting in order to develop an emergency vehicle proximity sensing system. This system prepares the alert messages, an emergency vehicle transmitter, an antenna for digital radio broadcast transmission, and a digital radio broadcast receiver. It is important to denote that the vehicle transmitter attains a digital radio broadcast transmission at a predetermined FM or AM frequency.

Additionally, an Emergency Traffic Information System is demonstrated in the work of Kubat et al. (2012). The major feature of this system is that the alert messages are sent within the FM broadcast band using RDS (Radio Data System) technology.

Finally, a DRM emergency information system is presented in the study of Shabrina (2017). The study doesn't direct attention to system design, but focuses attention on the system's coverage in the light of a specific methodology. It is essential to point up that the respective DRM emergency information system achieved a 99% coverage percentage.

The studies mentioned refer to emergency information systems which deliver emergency messages digitally despite the technology used for signal transmission. In the light of these technologies, our approach focuses on developing an emergency information system taking advantage of the avails of the DRM digital transmission and digital message delivery process.

Emergency Information System Development

The Uniwa-EIS System

We are currently working on developing an Emergency Information System by the use of appropriate technology which is available in remote areas. On account of the problems related to digital means and the need for modulation techniques (Kang & Choo, 2016; Proloy et al., 2017; Forstmann et al., 2011), we are working on developing an emergency information system based on the avails of DRM technology (Ellingson, 2016). It is important to highlight these avails, stressing the great signal coverage (no radio broadcast repeaters are required) and the economically affordable signal reception (no providers needed). In more detail, our approach is focused on designing an Emergency Information System in a way that the emergency content will be delivered accurately and rapidly (Jang et al., 2009). Our objective is also centered on designing a stable system which will achieve the maximum coverage percentage in areas featured by rough geographical terrain. To this end, our system design was based on the DRM EWF standards. Our system, which is called "UNIWA-EIS," is illustrated in Figure 1.

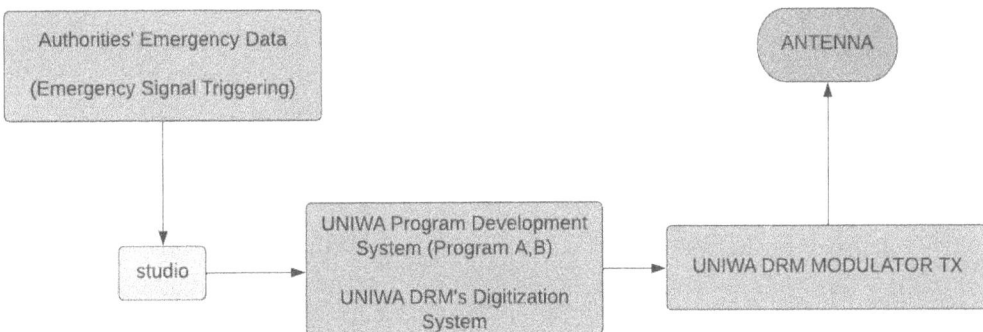

Figure 1. The UNIWA-EIS system.

The principal units of our system are:

1. A Program Development System which is a remotely controlled system that develops the respective programs based on the emergency content;

2. A DRM Digitization System which encodes the emergency content;

3. A DRM Modulation/ Broadcasting System which broadcasts the encoded emergency content.

It is also important to emphasize that our system is facilitated with fixed-line internet, mobile internet living up to 4G and 5G standards along with satellite internet. Additionally, our system uses alternative, environmentally-friendly power sources.

As depicted in Figure 1, the entire process includes the following stages:

1. The signal which is triggered by authorities is transferred into the studio and is activated at the UNIWA-Content Server.

2. The UNIWA Content Server develops the respective program which is about to be broadcast by a proper DRM modulator. It is essential to explain that the Program Development System is incorporated into the Content Server, and it is held responsible for developing the appropriate program with respect to the selected DRM service. It is important to denote that the DRM Digitization System is also a part of the Content Server and it encodes the emergency content.

It is vital to point out that the 'SPARK' software which meets the DRM's standards has been used in the program development process on the content server.

Testing our system

Our objective was to test the coverage of our system in areas featured by rough geographical terrain. For this purpose, our system came into effect in the region of Vigla, an area located on the island of Symi. Vigla was selected due to its specific morphology. The coverage study was based on the philosophy of a standard methodology called "LEG-BAC" (Mattson, 2005). This methodology provides coverage results by analyzing valuable data such as those listed below:

• Site longitude;

• Site latitude;

• Transmitter Power;

• Carrier Wave Frequency.

The area of Vigla is defined as the 'Site' in our case. The respective data was collected and analyzed by means of proper software. It is important to point out that transmitter power and site longitude and latitude were parameters which were also used in the study of Shabrina (2017) to test the coverage of a DRM emergency information system.

It is vital to illustrate that, in line with the study of Shabrina (2017), we carried out the coverage test in four phases. These phases were different in terms of the antenna central frequency and the antenna polarization (horizontal/vertical). However, the transmitter power value was the same in all phases (586 Watt). The results proved that a slight adjustment to these antenna characteristics didn't significantly alter the coverage percentage.

Results

The analysis outcome is well depicted in Figure 2. The map illustrated in this figure shows the coverage calibration (phases). Table 1 presents the antenna adjustment in each phase.

Table 1: Antenna's Adjustment

Phase	Antenna Central Frequency	Antenna Polarization
Phase 1	107.9	Horizontal
Phase 2	100	Vertical
Phase 3	104.6	Horizontal
Phase 4	88.2	Vertical

Each phase is depicted on the map by the use of a different color. The red color depicts phase 1, the yellow color illustrates phase 2, the light blue color depicts phase 3 and the light magenta color illustrates phase 4. The coverage percentage in each phase is shown in the table on the right-hand side of the map. The system achieved the following coverage percentage according to the antenna settings in each phase. The coverage outcome is shown in Table 2.

Table 2: Coverage Percentage

Phase	Coverage Percentage
Phase 1	99.7
Phase 2	98.3
Phase 3	99.2
Phase 4	98.1

Thereby, our system reached a 98.8 coverage percentage.

Figure 2. Coverage details.

Discussion

It is important to stress the fact that the study of Shabrina (2017) has tested the coverage of a DRM emergency information system in the area of Indonesia and the coverage score (99%) proved that this system works well in that region. It is also essential to stress the fact that in this study the coverage percentage varied according to the antenna adjustment and the antenna type. In particular, the coverage percentage was significantly altered with the antenna adjustment. It is essential to indicate that in the stages where the antenna central frequency changed noticeably, the coverage percentage dropped to 93%. In our case, the coverage outcome proved that our system achieved a high coverage percentage in each antenna features adjustment phase, indicating that the coverage percentage was not significantly affected by the antenna calibration. Even in stage 4, where the lowest coverage percentage was observed, the respective percentage didn't drop significantly (98.1). Additionally, the coverage test in the study of Shabrina (2017) was not based on the ground morphology of Indonesia and the system was not tested in cases of remote areas. On the contrary, our system has been tested in an area featured by rough geographical terrain, proving its robustness. Finally, the high coverage percentage proved that our system works well in remote areas with rough geographical features, indicating that such a system could be used to efficiently transmit the emergency content in the respective areas offsetting a liable internet failure (Jang et al., 2009). Our team is currently working on testing the coverage potential of our system by making further adjustments to the antenna in order to come up with extra parameters in view of examining their effect on the system coverage.

Conclusion

This paper focuses on the technologies which could be employed in order to develop emergency information systems and places emphasis on the design of a competent DRM emergency information system which works well in areas featured by rough geographical landscape. The paper also demonstrates a specific framework to test the coverage of such a system. The system was put into action and the results were promising. The high coverage score indicates that DRM emergency information systems appear to work well in remote areas. Nevertheless, more studies are needed to display the defects of such systems in these areas.

References

Bai Y., Duh W., Ma Z., Shen C., Zhou Y., & Chen B. (2010). Emergency communication system by heterogeneous wireless networking. In *Proceedings of the IEEE Intern.l Conf on Wireless Communications Networking and Information Security.*

Bartel, V.D.W., Murray, T., & Starr, R.H. (Eds.) (2009).

Information systems for emergency management (Advances in Management Information Systems). Taylor & Francis.

Choi, K.S. & Lee S. P. (2008). A proposal of the national disaster emergency satellite communications networking. *In Proceedings of the ICACT,* 396-399.

Deng L., Hinton G.., & Kingsbury, B. (2013). New types of deep neural network learning for speech recognition and related applications: An overview. *IEEE Int. Conf. on Acoustics, Speech and Signal Proc.,* 8599– 8603.

El-Dinary, A. (2018). *Systems and Methods for Emergency Vehicle Proximity Warning Using Digital Radio Broadcast.* United States Patent. Pub. No. US 9, 986, 401 B2.

Ellingson, S.W. (2016). *Radio Systems Engineering.* Cambridge University Press.

Endsley, M. R., Bolte, B., & Jones, D. G. (2011). *Designing for situation awareness: An approach to human-centered design* (2nd ed.). Taylor & Francis.

Jennex, M. E. (2007). *Modeling emergency response systems.* In H. I. Waikoloa (Ed.),

Proceedings of the 40ᵗʰ Annual Hawaii International Conference on system sciences (HICSS 2007). IEEE Computer Society.

Kang, B., & Choo, H. (2016). A deep-learning based emergency alert system. *ICT Express, 2*(2), 67-70.

Khalid M., &Shafiai S. (2015). Flood Disaster Management in Malaysia: An Evaluation of the Effectiveness Flood Delivery System. *Journal of Social Science and Humanity,* 5(4), 398-402.

Kubát, D., Kviz, J., Skrbek J., &Žižka, T. (2012). *Distributing Emergency Traffic Information.* 20ᵗʰ IDMT Conference.

Kumbhar, A., & Guvenc, I. (2015, April). A Comparative Study of Land Mobile Radio and LTE-based Public Safety Communications. *IEEE Southeast Conference.* DOI: 10.13140/ RG.2.1.2687.9528.

Le, Q.V., Ngiam, J., Coates, A., Lahiri, A., Prochnow, B., & Ng, A.Y. (2011). On optimization methods for deep learning. *Proceedings of the 28th International Conference on Machine Learning (ICML-11),* 265–272.

Lien, Y., Jang, H., & Chail, T. (2009). A MANET Based Emergency Communication and Information System for Catastrophic Natural Disasters. *9th IEEE International Conforonco on Distributcd Computing Systcms Workshops,* 412-417, dui. 10.1109/ICDCSW.2009.72

Mattsson, A. (2005). Single frequency networks in DTV. *IEEE transactions on broadcasting,* 51(4), 413-422.

Proloy, R., Ahmed, S., & Hossain, A. (2017). Comparative Analysis of Various Wireless Digital Modulation Techniques with different Channel Coding Schemes under AWGN Channel. *International Journal of Computer Applications (0975 – 8887),* 161(3), 30-34.

Ridderinkhof K., Forstmann, B.U., Wylie, S.A., Burle, B., & van den Wildenberg, W.P.M. (2011). Neurocognitive mechanisms of action control: Resisting the call of the sirens. *Wiley Interdiscip. Rev. Cogn. Sci., 2* (2), 174–192.

Shabrina, N. H. (2017). Simulation of Digital Radio Mondiale (DRM) Coverage Prediction–A study case with Radio Republic Indonesia (RRI). *IJNMT (International Journal of New Media Technology),* 4(1), 32-36.

Siergiejczyk, M. (2015). Analysis Of The Analogue And Digital Cooperation Of

The Railway Radio Communications in the Context of the Emergency Call. *Journal of KONES Powertrain and Transport, 22*(4), 253-268.

Stadelmeier, L., Kan, M., Loghin, D., Schneider, J., Ner, I., Lachlan, B., Shinohara, Y., Atungsiri, S., Gholam, H., & Taylor M. (2016). *Transmitter and Transmission Method for Transmitting Payload Data and Emergency Information. United States Patent Application. Pub. No. US 2016/0094895 A1.*

Sutskever, I., Martens J., Dahl, G.., & Hinton, G. (2013). On the importance of initialization and momentum in deep learning. *Proceedings of the 30th International Conference on Machine Learning,* ICML-13, 1139–1147.

Tarchi D., Fantacci, R., & Marabissi D. (2009). The communication infrastructure for emergency management: The integrated system for emergency vision. *Proceedings of IWCMC,* 618-622. https://doi.org/10.1145/1582379.1582513

Tubtiang, A. (2005, February 28). *Role of ICT for Disaster Reduction.* APT-ITU Joint Meeting. Bangkok, Thailand.

Velazquez, L., & Ford, J. (2012). *Methods and Apparatus for Transmitting Emergency Alert Messages.* United States Patent Application. Pub. No. US 8,250,598 B2.

Journal on Policy and Complex Systems • Volume 7, Number 2 • Fall 2021

A Return to "A Complexity Context to Classroom Interactions and Climate Impact on Achievement"

Joseph Cochran

The College at Brockport, State University of New York

Liz Johnson

*The University of North Carolina Charlotte
& Complex Systems Institute*

ABSTRACT

When JPCS published "A Complexity Context to Classroom Interactions and Climate Impact on Achievement" in 2017, the article was a cutting-edge application of ABM to classroom dynamics.
Five years later, though, there have been dramatic changes to education as a result of the COVID-19 pandemic. While the technology of ABM has advanced sufficiently that reexamining of the
topic may be justified, the trauma caused by the pandemic should
make us question whether any such model would accurately reflect
the real world. Given the isolating nature of COVID-19 and online
learning, the purpose of this article is to remind us that in a classroom environment, "every interaction matters." Effective action
steps can easily be taken to dramatically strengthen interactions
and thus strengthen leaning networks, which will lead to higher
levels of achievement. This can be done by the means of simple
strategies like increasing positive climate behavioral markers in the
classroom, like using student names, checking-in with students,
smiling, using polite language, laughing, and clapping. In contrast,
negative behavior markers like anger, sarcasm, irritability, harsh
voice, yelling, exclusion of students, bad language, physical control
of students, teasing, and bullying must be eradicated.

Keywords: complexity, classroom environment, interactions, networks, COVID-19, dragon kings

doi: 10.18278/jpcs.7.2.6

Un regreso a "Un contexto de complejidad para las interacciones en el aula y el impacto climático en el rendimiento"

Resumen

Cuando JPCS publicó "Un contexto de complejidad para las interacciones en el aula y el impacto climático en el rendimiento" en 2017, el artículo fue una aplicación de vanguardia de ABM a la dinámica del aula. Sin embargo, cinco años después, ha habido cambios dramáticos en la educación como resultado de la pandemia de COVID-19. Si bien la tecnología de ABM ha avanzado lo suficiente como para que se justifique reexaminar el tema, el trauma causado por la pandemia debería hacernos cuestionar si algún modelo de este tipo reflejaría con precisión el mundo real. Dada la naturaleza aislante del COVID-19 y el aprendizaje en línea, el propósito de este artículo es recordarnos que en el ambiente de un salón de clases, "todas las interacciones son importantes". Se pueden tomar fácilmente pasos de acción efectivos para fortalecer dramáticamente las interacciones y, por lo tanto, fortalecer las redes de aprendizaje, lo que conducirá a niveles más altos de logro. Esto se puede hacer por medio de estrategias simples como aumentar los marcadores de comportamiento de clima positivo en el aula como: usar los nombres de los estudiantes, registrarse con los estudiantes, sonreír, usar un lenguaje cortés, reír y aplaudir. Por el contrario, se deben erradicar los marcadores de comportamiento negativo como la ira, el sarcasmo, la irritabilidad, la voz áspera, los gritos, la exclusión de los estudiantes, el lenguaje soez, el control físico de los estudiantes, las burlas y el acoso.

Palabras clave: complejidad, ambiente de aula, interacciones, redes, COVID-19

重审《复杂情境：课堂互动和课堂气氛对成绩产生的影响》

摘要

当《政策与复杂系统杂志》于2017年发表《复杂情境：课堂互动和课堂气氛对成绩产生的影响》一文时，该文是基于Agent模型（ABM）应用于课堂动态的最新案例。5年后，因

2019冠状病毒病（COVID-19）大流行的影响，教育发生了显著变革。尽管ABM技术已有了充足的进步，让对该主题进行再分析一事具备合理性，但大流行造成的创伤让我们质疑这类模型是否能精确反映现实世界。鉴于COVID-19和网络学习的孤立性质，本文旨在提醒我们，在课堂环境中，"一切互动都至关重要"。（教师）能轻松采取有效的行动步骤，以显著加强互动，并因此增强学习网络，进而将导致更高的学习成绩。此举能通过一系列简单策略完成，例如增加积极的课堂气氛行为标记，包括使用学生姓名、问候学生、微笑、使用礼貌语言、大笑、以及鼓掌。相反，消极的行为标记，例如愤怒、讥讽、易怒、厉声、吼叫、排斥学生、不良语言、对学生进行身体控制、嘲笑和霸凌等行为必须被消除

关键词：复杂性，课堂环境，互动，网络，2019冠状病毒病

Introduction

Within the complexity science literature, there is the concept of the Dragon King (See Figure 1), which is a massive event that comes from unique origins (Ricci & Sheng, 2017). The size of Dragon Kings makes them 'kings' while their uniqueness makes them 'dragons.' They arise from wickedly complex feedback loops that align to multiply the impact of the events that feed the developing Dragon King. When Dragon Kings are finally 'born,' the largest can change the course of human history through the devastation that they cause, though smaller Dragon Kings exist.

The COVID-19 pandemic is among the largest Dragon Kings in recent history because of its economic and social impact. Its economic impact is at least $10 trillion, though it will likely be decades before its true economic consequences can be determined. Its social impact is equally large because it is the fifth most deadly pandemic in human history, having possibly killed over twenty million people globally. Within the USA, it is the single largest mass casualty event in American history, as its nearly one million fatalities exceed the death tolls of any other mass casualty event in US history.

We would consider the COVID-19 pandemic a Dragon King because it benefited from a unique combination of factors that allowed it to be the first global pandemic of the 21st century. It benefited from the fact that it arose in Wuhan during late 2019, when the local officials were unwilling to take steps to deal with a potential pandemic because of political reasons. It benefited from a global trade network more extensive than any that had existed in the 20th century, which allowed it to spread quickly throughout the world. It benefited from the fact that conservatives in the American and European continents were unwilling to initially quarantine their populations due to concerns about the impact on their national economies. Finally, it benefitted from a massive amount of disinformation and misinformation spread through social media.

Generic Prediction Phase Diagram

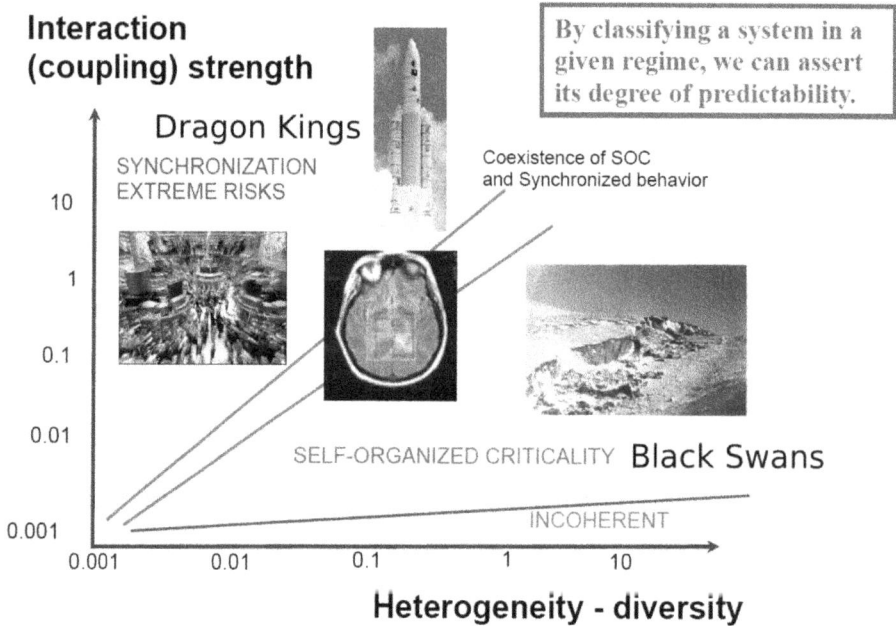

Figure 1. Predictability based on interaction and diversity in a system (Sornette, 2009).

Education

When it came to education, the COVID-19 pandemic resulted in challenges that administrators, parents, students, and teachers were not prepared to meet. Within the USA, the entire education system shifted from primarily in-person to exclusively virtual in just a couple of months, disrupting the education of students and destroying the engagement that they had developed within the classroom. Suddenly, students were physically disengaged from their peers and their teachers, which had dramatic consequences on their educational performance and their psychological well-being.

No published study could have predicted the impact of the pandemic because no journal would have published such an exploration. Before COVID-19, the only successful pandemic in the last half century had been the HIV/AIDS pandemic, which had only been able to spread and survive because it did not cause visible symptoms during the first couple of years of infection, allowing an infected person to spread it to other people before they started to show symptoms of the sickness. Pandemics of the type that COVID-19 represented had been defeated by modern medicine, so they were not worth modeling, especially when it came to the field of education.

The previous three years have shown us the error of our arrogance, that technology can just as effectively spread a pandemic as it can prevent it, especially when people do not care about the consequences of their decisions and/or lack an understanding of basic science. When workers are unwilling to wear masks or to accept vaccination when they know that they will face termination of employment, it suggests that society has failed on some fundamental level. The only question becomes the source of the failure.

Since the pandemic occurred, though, there is an opportunity for researchers to not only model rare events, but to also model failures of society. The pandemic revealed massive failures within American society, primarily related to decades of reduced taxation for the middle and upper classes, decades of reduced services for the working and lower classes, and decades of worship for the corporation. The American education system suffers from each of these failures, as conservative governments have reduced funding for public schools so that they could afford tax cuts for the wealthy and so that they could reduce the quality of public schools so that the public would support the privatization of the education system.

Due to the failures of American society, the American education system broke during the pandemic years. Most American school systems were not equipped with the technology required for virtual teaching and most American teachers were not trained in remote pedagogy. Even when they were, many families lacked the resources for computers for every member of the house and/or the high-quality internet connections required to support multiple family members engaging in video conferencing at the same time, meaning that many students effectively became home schooled, as they were forced to do work asynchronously.

Modeling Crises

While the impact of the COVID-19 pandemic far exceeds the impact of most crises, there will always be some crisis or another that will impact students. With each crisis, students and teachers will find that classroom interactions and climate are negatively impacted, meaning that any model should account for the impact of exogenous factors. Otherwise, the model will have limited predictive utility.

As we examine the model of the paper, we see what could be considered a good 'status quo' model, which is the standard for most models because global crises are difficult to predict and tend to overwhelm predictive models. Before 2020, it was also accepted wisdom that any global pandemic that evolved would probably mimic the slow progression of the HIV/AIDS pandemic, so it would not have a significant impact on most predictive models (except in communities where HIV/AIDS infection rates exceeded 1%). When researchers bothered to model global crises, they were much more likely to focus on highly predictable events such as global climate change rather than highly unpredictable events such as pandemics.

While a 'status quo' model was sufficient for 2017, the pandemic has shown that such models are insufficient for reflecting real life, as 'global crisis' models are needed to have a chance of accurate predictions. Within the field of education, a 'global crisis' model would attempt to model the impact of shifting from an in-person and synchronous education system to a remote and/or asynchronous education system. Such a model could represent the impact of a 'global crisis' on every level of education, from elementary school to doctoral programs, though more advanced students would presumably have more resilience than less advanced students.

A 'global crisis' model would randomly assign every agent a value for a triggered anxiety variable and a triggered depression variable. When randomly triggered within the ABM model, the global crisis would cause a 'physical' separation of students and their teachers and students and their peers, removing the possibility of in-person interactions between students and teachers and students and their peers. It would also activate the triggered anxiety variable and the triggered depression variable.

Anxiety is important because it represents the inhibition of the development of a positive classroom climate. Teachers that experience anxiety will be incapable of facilitating a positive classroom climate while students that experienced anxiety will be incapable of responding to a positive classroom climate. In classrooms where teachers and students suffer from low anxiety levels, the climate would end up being more positive than in classrooms where teachers and students suffer from high anxiety levels.

Depression is also important because it represents the inhibition of the development of positive classroom interactions. Teachers that experience depression will be incapable of engaging students in a fashion that will develop positive relationships with their students while students that experience depression will be incapable of engaging their peers in a fashion that will develop positive relationships with their peers. In classrooms where teachers and students suffer from low depression levels, there would be more positive interactions than in classrooms where teachers and students suffer from high depression levels.

By examining the impact of global crises on classroom interactions and climate through anxiety and depression, it would be possible to assess their effects on student achievement. This means that it should be possible to model the impact of the COVID-19 pandemic on student achievement in the USA through using ABM. The impact of anxiety and depression on student achievement could also be evaluated outside of global crises, as anxiety and depression are the most common psychological difficulties experienced by human beings.

Modeling Improvements

If the researchers of the article were willing to do subsequent research using ABM to assess impacts on student achievement, they would be well served to include a 'global crisis' models, as well as their 'status quo' models. 'Global crisis' models would potentially improve the accuracy and generalizability of their research because they would account for the impact of exogenous events on student achievement. Even if they do not cause the physical separation that was experienced by the COVID-19 pandemic, global crises will likely trigger anxiety and depression in a significant percentage of the population, which will influence anxiety and depression in students and teacher.

Another possible suggestion for modeling improvement would be to include an 'expanded crisis' model, where the anxiety and depression of the students and teachers are influenced by the anxiety and depression of the people in their lives. Since no human being is an island, the anxiety and depression of people in their lives would likely increase the anxiety and depression experienced by students and teachers. By doing so, it would be possible to model how the impact of a global crisis on a community would affect student achievement.

If the models showed that the anxiety and depression caused by a global crisis significantly decreased student achievement, it would suggest that governments should consider a more proactive efforts to address the psychological consequences of global crises. Since student achievement is directly related to educational attainment and educational attainment is directly related to future success, any reduction to student achievement could have a long-term impact on the economic prosperity of individuals. Since the economic prosperity of a societies are the sum of the economic prosperity of individuals, they could also have a long-term impact on the economic prosperity of societies.

Teaching Improvements

It seems the online challenges of teaching further exacerbated the creation of a positive classroom environment. Given the "wickedly complex feedback loops" from the Dragon King analogy, what can be done? Furthermore, once positive feedback loops are created how can negative consequences be eradicated? First most teachers, are not fully aware of the factors that comprise classroom climate and how powerful their roles as teachers can be in terms of interactions, network strengthening, and acknowledging depression/anxiety. Furthermore, few teachers know what their classroom climate is or are aware of how students emotionally experience their classroom. Given the fragile state of some students and teachers, negative behavioral markers like anger, sarcasm, irritability, harsh voice, yelling, exclusion of students, bad language, physical control of students, teasing, and bullying must be acknowledged and eradicated. This can be done through awareness and assessment. Climate, interrelating factors, and corresponding outcomes are advantageous to examine so that teachers can recognize that changes in their leadership affect their classes' learning environments and come up with better ways to account for isolation and emotional challenges (Johnson, 2015).

Through a complexity context, researchers can provide details on the dynamics of classroom interactions as to strengthen and sustain the classroom so as to strengthen the entire system. Freiberg (1999) argued that research has not adequately addressed classroom processes of change dynamics in relation to the collective impact of processes on student achievement outcomes. "Teachers operate within a complex ecosystem of factors that contribute to (or impede) teaching and learning" (Starr & Weiss, 2015, para. 4). A noncomplexity approach has been the standard in attempts to solve climate and achievement. However, a complexity context accommodates the nonlinear relationships, bidirectional feedback loops, and time-delayed effects, which are key elements of classroom interactions that can further leverage achievement (Mabry et al., 2013). For example, standardized objective and specific feedback from classroom climate assessments and classroom observations (See Table 1-1) of visible behavior markers is a starting point. First, this process involves knowing exactly what the climate is as a starting point to employ a pre-test post-test strategy. Repeating the process over time, and

taking into account depression/anxiety, can provide more accurate feedback and trend lines to induce achievement outcomes (Johnson, 2015).

Yet what would the optimal climate in a global crisis be and what patterns of interactions could the teacher employ for positive sustainability? Important to consider is students' input on their classroom climate, given that students and teachers co-create their environment together. For example, teachers can easily solicit feedback from students on what they imagine an ideal classroom should be. This can be done through standardized research instruments (like the CES Ideal classroom survey, Trickett & Moos, 2002) or informally through assignments. Repetition of the process can provide even more valuable feedback to assess if the ideal is working or what adaptations are needed.

Additionally, teachers can create their own classroom climate feedback assessments by video recording instructional sessions in their classroom. For instance, a half hour session can provide novel feedback data even if students work on their own for part of the class. Next, teachers can count specific categories of instructional, emotionally supportive, and behavioral management interactions (See Table 1). First count the totals of all-instructional, emotionally supportive, and behavioral management interactions. Next taking a percentage of each can measure can determine the rate of instructional interactions that occur in a half hour. Teachers can then begin to determine how the rate of instruction varies depending on type of instruction, delivery method, and varied ways students can be engaged and corresponding impact on academic achievement. Next teachers can explore how emotionally supportive and behavioral management interrelate and identify possible patterns that lead to more effectiveness (Johnson, 2016).

Table 1. Classroom Assessment Scoring System (CLASS): 10 Dimensions Linked to Student Achievement (Pianta, 2012)

Emotional support — the way teachers help children develop warm, supportive relationships, experience enjoyment and excitement about learning, feel comfortable in the classroom, and experience appropriate levels of autonomy or independence

Positive climate — the enjoyment and emotional connection that teachers have with students, as well as the nature of their interactions

Negative climate — the level of expressed negativity such as anger, hostility, or aggression exhibited by teachers or students in the classroom

Teacher sensitivity — teachers' responsiveness to students' academic and emotional needs

Regard for student perspectives — the degree to which teachers' interactions with students and classroom activities place an emphasis on students' interests, motivations, and points of view

---

Classroom organization — the way teachers help children develop skills to regulate their own behavior, get the most learning out of each school day, and maintain interest in learning activities

Behavior management — how well teachers monitor, prevent, and redirect misbehavior

Productivity — how well the classroom runs with respect to routines, how well students understand the routine, and the degree to which teachers provide activities and directions so that maximum time can be spent in leaning activities

Instructional learning formats — how teachers engage students in activities and facilitate activities so that leaning opportunities are maximized

---

Instructional support — the ways in which teachers effectively support students' cognitive development and language growth

Concept development — how teachers use instructional discussions and activities to promote students' higher order thinking skills and cognition in contrast to a focus on rote instruction

Quality of feedback — how teachers expand participation and learning through feedback to students

Language modeling — the extent to which teachers stimulate, facilitate, and encourage students' language use

---

Also, teachers can work on strategies to incorporate more emotionally supportive interactions that contribute to creating and sustaining a positive climate and that do not take valuable time away from instruction. For example, using the names of all students, moving toward every student, using polite language, smiling, laughing, and checking in with students to see if they are understanding the instructional interactions contribute to the co-creation of a positive learning environment. However, there is no guarantee all students will grasp instruction given (Johnson, 2016). Though, teachers have the power to activate interaction strategies for facilitative conditions for sustaining a positive climate, which research has demonstrated can increase average achievement scores up to 25% (CASTL, n.d.).

Once positive feedback loops are created sustaining a positive classroom environment, strategies to diminish negative consequences must be adopted. For example, there can be a positive learning environment but not much learning happens. As the saying goes, "you can lead a horse to water but cannot make them drink." The process of learning systems feedback needs to include student agency, student-regulation, and self-assessment feedback. According to Stiggens (2008), the most critical instructional decisions with the most impact on student success, are made by the students themselves. Self-feedback is beneficial to students because they tend to discover more value in their learning and take more ownership (Brookhart, Moss, & Long, 2009). Loveless (2022) claims student

self-assessment is simple, whereby students need to determine what they were supposed to learn, did they learn it, and do they have any additional questions. For example, see Figure 2 below.

This type of approach could prove even more effective with "immediate" feedback with technology like an app, that funnels data directly to instructors so they can adapt to meet students' learning needs in a timely fashion. This is a research direction we propose to further explore. Certainly, this approach will not prevent all negative consequences. However, this type of feedback loop is flexible, effective, and easy to apply (Leahy et al., 2005).

Suggestions for Future Research

Future researchers should consider including Dragon Kings in their models when using ABM, as doing so would improve the accuracy and generalizability of their models. While Dragon Kings are rare phenomena, they can produce global crises that change human society, meaning that they will limit the utility of any research that does not attempt to account for their impacts. By not accounting for the existence of possible Dragon Kings, researchers do themselves a disservice because they limit the accuracy and the generalizability of their studies.

While the COVID-19 pandemic will eventually end, there will be other global crises, especially as global climate change continues its progression due to the shortsightedness of world leaders. Dragon Kings will continue

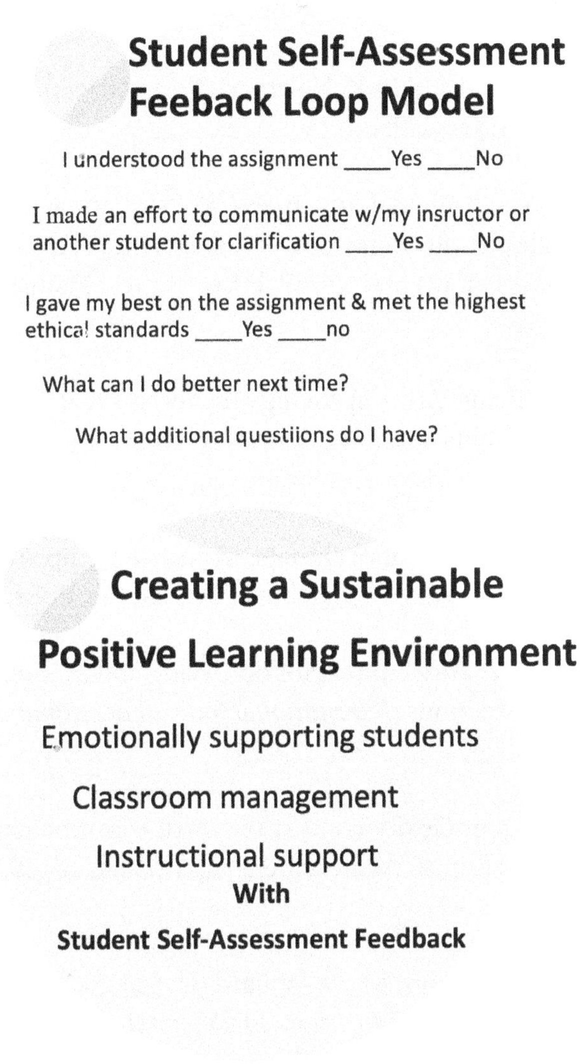

Student Self-Assessment
Feeback Loop Model

I understood the assignment ____Yes ____No

I made an effort to communicate w/my insructor or
another student for clarification ____Yes ____No

I gave my best on the assignment & met the highest
ethical standards ____Yes ____no

What can I do better next time?

What additional questiions do I have?

Creating a Sustainable
Positive Learning Environment

Emotionally supporting students

Classroom management

Instructional support
With
Student Self-Assessment Feedback

Figure 2. Student self-assessment feedback model interrelating with
elements of creating a sustainable positive learning environment.

to arise from the mistakes of humanity, whether they were caused by avarice, ignorance, or malice, and they will disrupt human society. Of course, researchers will need to clearly state their assumptions concerning their modeling, as different types of global crises will have different impacts on the population. As Bethune implored, "we must have the courage to change old ideas and practices" (Bethune, 2000, p. 395). Finally, teachers must deal with uncontrollable influences from outside the classroom. They have agency and power to create a positive or negative climate by their verbal and nonverbal interactions. Teachers' interactions have consequences that impact students' achievement, emotional states, and students' lives. Consequently, every interaction matters (Johnson, 2016).

References

Bethune, M. M. (2000). Youth. In R. Newman (Ed.), African American quotations (p. 395). New York, NY: Oryx Press.

Brookhart, S. M., Moss, C. M., & Long, B. A. (2009). Promoting student ownership of learning through high-impact formative assessment practices. *Journal of Multi-Disciplinary Evaluation*, 6(12), pp. 52–67. https://journals.sfu.ca/jmde/index.php/jmde_1/article/view/234

CASTL. (n.d.). Measuring and improving teacher-student interactions in PK-12 setting to enhance students' learning. Retrieved December 18, 2015, from http://curry.virginia.edu/uploads/resourceLibrary/CLASS-MTP_PK-12_brief.pdf

Freiberg, H. J. (Ed.). (1999). School climate: Measuring, improving and sustaining healthy learning environments. Philadelphia, PA: Falmer Press.

Johnson, L. (2015). A network context for observing and mapping of Ghana mathematics classroom interactions. *International Journal of Humanities and Social Science, 5*(1), 1-19.

Johnson, L. (2016). A complexity context to North Carolina charter school classroom interactions and climate: Achievement gap impacts (#13035) [Doctorial dissertation]. ProQuest.

Leahy, S., Lyon, C., Thompson, M., & Wiliam, D. (2005). Classroom assessment: Minute by minute, day by day. *Educational Leadership (63)*, 3, pp. 18-24.

Loveless, B. (2022). Helping students thrive by using self-assessment. Education Corner. https://www.educationcorner.com/helping-students-self-assessment.html

Mabry, P. L., Milstein, B., Abraido-Lanza, A. F., Livingood, W. C., & Allegrante, J. P. (2013). Opening a window on systems science research in health promotion and public health. *Society for Public Health Education, 40*(1S). doi: 10.1177/1090198113503343

Pianta, R. C. (2012). CLASS dimensions guide. Charlottesville, VA: Teachstone Training LLC.

Ricci, P.F. & Sheng, H.-X. (2017). Accessing catastrophes-Dragon Kings, Black, and Gray Swans-for science-policy. *Global Challenges, 1*(6), n/a. https://doi.org/10.1002/gch2.201700021

Sornette, D. (2009). Dragon-kings, black swans and the prediction crisis. *International Journal of Terraspace Science and Engineering* (2). pp.1-19.

Starr, J. & Weiss, E. (2015). 5 questions policymakers need to ask about Common-Core test results. Education Week. Retrieved from http: www.edweek.org/ew/articles/2015/10/07/5-questions-policymakers-need-toask-about.html

Stiggins, R. J. (2008). *Student-involved assessment FOR learning.* Pearson Merrill Prentice Hall.

Trickett, E. J., & Moos, R. H. (2002). A social climate scale (3rd ed.). Menlo Park, CA: Mind Garden.

Related Titles from Westphalia Press

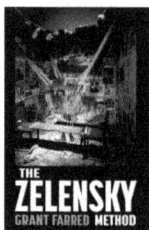

The Zelensky Method
by Grant Farred

Locating Russian's war within a global context, The Zelensky Method is unsparing in its critique of those nations, who have refused to condemn Russia's invasion and are doing everything they can to prevent economic sanctions from being imposed on the Kremlin.

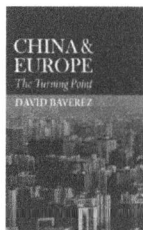

China & Europe: The Turning Point
by David Baverez

In creating five fictitious conversations between Xi Jinping and five European experts, David Baverez, who lives and works in Hong Kong, offers up a totally new vision of the relationship between China and Europe.

Masonic Myths and Legends
by Pierre Mollier

Freemasonry is one of the few organizations whose teaching method is still based on symbols. It presents these symbols by inserting them into legends that are told to its members in initiation ceremonies. But its history itself has also given rise to a whole mythology.

Resistance: Reflections on Survival, Hope and Love
Poetry by William Morris, Photography by Jackie Malden

Resistance is a book of poems with photographs or a book of photographs with poems depending on your perspective. The book is comprised of three sections titled respectively: On Survival, On Hope, and On Love.

Bunker Diplomacy: An Arab-American in the U.S. Foreign Service
by Nabeel Khoury

After twenty-five years in the Foreign Service, Dr. Nabeel A. Khoury retired from the U.S. Department of State in 2013 with the rank of Minister Counselor. In his last overseas posting, Khoury served as deputy chief of mission at the U.S. embassy in Yemen (2004-2007).

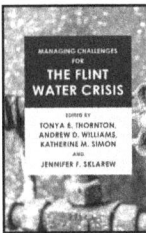

Managing Challenges for the Flint Water Crisis
Edited by Toyna E. Thornton, Andrew D. Williams, Katherine M. Simon, Jennifer F. Sklarew

This edited volume examines several public management and intergovernmental failures, with particular attention on social, political, and financial impacts. Understanding disaster meaning, even causality, is essential to the problem-solving process.

Donald J. Trump, The 45th U.S. Presidency and Beyond International Perspectives
Editors: John Dixon and Max J. Skidmore

The reality is that throughout Trump's presidency, there was a clearly perceptible decline of his—and America's—global standing, which accelerated as an upshot of his mishandling of both the Corvid-19 pandemic and his 2020 presidential election loss.

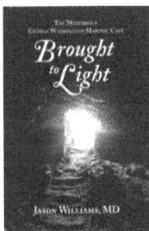

Brought to Light: The Mysterious George Washington Masonic Cave
by Jason Williams, MD

The George Washington Masonic Cave near Charles Town, West Virginia, contains a signature carving of George Washington dated 1748. Although this inscription appears authentic, it has yet to be verified by historical accounts or scientific inquiry.

Abortion and Informed Common Sense
by Max J. Skidmore

The controversy over a woman's "right to choose," as opposed to the numerous "rights" that abortion opponents decide should be assumed to exist for "unborn children," has always struck me as incomplete. Two missing elements of the argument seems obvious, yet they remain almost completely overlooked.

The Athenian Year Primer: Attic Time-Reckoning and the Julian Calendar
by Christopher Planeaux

The ability to translate ancient Athenian calendar references into precise Julian-Gregorian dates will not only assist Ancient Historians and Classicists to date numerous historical events with much greater accuracy but also aid epigraphists in the restorations of numerous Attic inscriptions.

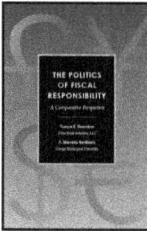

The Politics of Fiscal Responsibility: A Comparative Perspective
by Tonya E. Thornton and F. Stevens Redburn

Fiscal policy challenges following the Great Recession forced members of the Organisation for Economic Co-operation and Development (OECD) to implement a set of economic policies to manage public debt.

Growing Inequality: Bridging Complex Systems, Population Health, and Health Disparities
Editors: George A. Kaplan, Ana V. Diez Roux, Carl P. Simon, and Sandro Galea

Why is America's health is poorer than the health of other wealthy countries and why health inequities persist despite our efforts? In this book, researchers report on groundbreaking insights to simulate how these determinants come together to produce levels of population health and disparities and test new solutions.

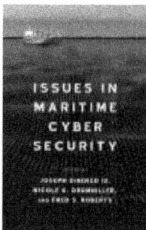

Issues in Maritime Cyber Security
Edited by Dr. Joe DiRenzo III, Dr. Nicole K. Drumhiller, and Dr. Fred S. Roberts

The complexity of making MTS safe from cyber attack is daunting and the need for all stakeholders in both government (at all levels) and private industry to be involved in cyber security is more significant than ever as the use of the MTS continues to grow.

A Radical In The East
by S. Brent Morris, PhD

The papers presented here represent over twenty-five years of publications by S. Brent Morris. They explore his many questions about Freemasonry, usually dealing with origins of the Craft. A complex organization with a lengthy pedigree like Freemasonry has many basic foundational questions waiting to be answered, and that's what this book does: answers questions.

Contests of Initiative: Countering China's Gray Zone Strategy in the East and South China Seas
by Dr. Raymond Kuo

China is engaged in a widespread assertion of sovereignty in the South and East China Seas. It employs a "gray zone" strategy: using coercive but sub-conventional military power to drive off challengers and prevent escalation, while simultaneously seizing territory and asserting maritime control.

Frontline Diplomacy: A Memoir of a Foreign Service Officer in the Middle East
by William A. Rugh

In short vignettes, this book describes how American diplomats working in the Middle East dealt with a variety of challenges over the last decades of the 20th century. Each of the vignettes concludes with an insight about diplomatic practice derived from the experience.

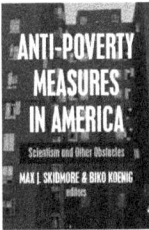

Anti-Poverty Measures in America: Scientism and Other Obstacles
Editors, Max J. Skidmore and Biko Koenig

Anti-Poverty Measures in America brings together a remarkable collection of essays dealing with the inhibiting effects of scientism, an over-dependence on scientific methodology that is prevalent in the social sciences, and other obstacles to anti-poverty legislation.

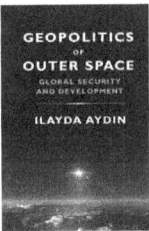

Geopolitics of Outer Space: Global Security and Development
by Ilayda Aydin

A desire for increased security and rapid development is driving nation-states to engage in an intensifying competition for the unique assets of space. This book analyses the Chinese-American space discourse from the lenses of international relations theory, history and political psychology to explore these questions.

westphaliapress.org

www.ingramcontent.com/pod-product-compliance
Lightning Source LLC
Chambersburg PA
CBHW061617210326
41520CB00041B/7486